SQL Programming

How To Learn SQL, The Practical Step-by-Step Guide. New Enhanced Learning Strategies In SQL Languages And Coding

By: Richard Numpy

Contents

Introduction

This book contains the important concepts, procedures, and steps you need to start designing, creating, and manipulating relational databases using the Structured Query Language (SQL).

SQL is the standard computer language for communicating with databases. It is a unique and simple, yet powerful language that you can use to store, filter, manipulate, and retrieve data to satisfy the present need for timely, relevant, and accurate information.

The Standard Query Language is more than just a language for retrieving data from databases. If you know how to make the most of it, you can start a rewarding career helping management and leaders make sound decisions. In an era when information is king, knowing how to deliver the information quickly, systematically, and efficiently is a huge advantage.

This book is an all-in-one resource that will help you learn SQL in no time at all. A beginner-friendly book was designed with both the beginner and intermediate users in mind.

The book "SQL Programming" is an excellent resource and workbook for beginners and intermediate learners who want to learn SQL in an effective and easy manner. It uses a combination of conceptual and practical approach to deliver intensive and comprehensive learning. It provides practice exercises that readers can use to test the theories and master the procedures.

This book provides in-depth step-by-step tutorial to help you set up a database, create tables efficiently from scratch or from existing tables, modify table structures, and create a copy of your tables. It shows how you can use SQL statements, clauses, keywords, and modifiers to retrieve and display data based on your requirements. It offers tons of interesting and relevant real world examples to demonstrate concepts and procedures.

It offers a collection of invaluable tips and techniques for designing useful and efficient databases. You will learn to construct tables that support data integrity and flexibility. You will know how to use constraints to ensure that you will be getting the kind of data you want to collect and work on. You will learn how to create virtual tables or views that you can use to help protect your data from being seen by unauthorized persons.

You will find practice exercises that you can work on to reinforce the concepts and skills you have learned.

You can use this book to discover the many effective ways of using a relational database to provide quick and useful information from multiple tables in a few lines of code. You will be in the best position to take advantage of its features and the career opportunities for jobs that require database administration and operation.

By the time you finish reading the book, you will have gained appreciation for SQL and its simple yet powerful commands. You will be equipped with the skills and knowledge that you can use to start a new career or enhance your current work prospects.

Chapter 1: Getting Familiar with SQL

Almost every computer application works with databases. Big and small organizations use relational database systems to run simple to complex tasks that involve tons of data in such fields as marketing, sales, production, and operations.

The Structured Query Language (SQL) is the standard computer language for interacting with relational database management systems. It enables users to access, store, retrieve, and manipulate data in relational databases. The most popular relational database management systems such as Microsoft SQL Server, Oracle, Ingres, and Access use SQL to efficiently manage and manipulate data and provide solutions to the data needs of various organizations.

Why Should You Use SQL?

A language that works with databases must provide functionalities that will allow users to take full advantages of the information at hand. It should enable fundamental actions such as creating, editing, maintaining data, and removing data. It has to allow users to access information from diverse sources quickly and easily. For the past decades, SQL has been efficiently and effectively meeting the needs of a vast number of organizations. It continues to evolve and improve and has proven to be a powerful, efficient, and flexible computer language.

Why is SQL the leading language for databases?

SQL has been the standard for database interaction and it has withstood the challenge of competitors through the years. It is a robust language that enjoys unrelenting support from communities of developers, programmers, and enthusiasts.

Database interfaces have improved tremendously in the past years and this can be attributed to the flexible nature of SQL.

Although it can work with the most complicated database systems, SQL itself has simple structures. It employs few, simple commands and conventions that are mainly definitional and manipulative. It even uses simple English words in its commands. For example, if you want to create a table, you can execute this simple statement: CREATE Table.

SQL uses other intuitive statements like ALTER Table, INSERT Into, etc. Its statements are also written in free format.

SQL is easy to learn and use. It offers relatively less learning curve and does not cost much to implement. Its command structures are easy to understand.

SQL enables large segments of an organization to efficiently utilize existing data for querying, data manipulation, and decision-making.

This powerful database language is capable of meeting the multi-faceted requirements of its users.

Nearly every database application today is powered by SQL. Developers and a large supportive community are proactively and continuously innovating on the functionalities of the language to suit the growing requirements for data and support the increasing complexities of running global businesses. This has resulted in the multiple variations and implementations of SQL.

Despite the massive growth, SQL versions have remained anchored on the standard ANSI-SQL, only allowing slight variations to respond to the specific needs of their users. This universality enables easy migration from one database application to another.

Is SQL a Programming Language?

While all developers and stakeholders will probably agree that Structured Query Language or SQL is a database management language for relational databases, there have been claims and counterclaims on its merits as a legitimate programming language.

Traditionalists or purists do not regard SQL as a programming language but acknowledge that its standards allow the creation of procedural extensions for itself, which allows it to function like standard programming languages.

This outlook appeared to have changed in recent times. Admittedly, SQL is not an imperative programming language. Imperative computer languages like BASIC and C tell the computer what to do and how to do something. On the other hand, SQL tells the computer what the user is looking for. Hence, many believe that in its standard state, it is fair to recognize SQL as a declarative programming language. Its extensions make SQL even more powerful by including the functionalities of a procedural programming language.

Summary:

The Structured Query Language (SQL) is the standard language for communicating with relational database management systems. Currently, it is widely regarded as a declarative programming language with extensions that enable it to work as a procedural programming language.

Chapter 2: Understanding Databases

If you are managing information in folders or files, you will likely realize that you have several files that store similar information. Quite possibly, you have several files on the same subject with unrelated information and you are having a rough time figuring out which file has the updated or accurate data. You may also find it exasperating to have to update several files to reflect even the minutest changes in information. You will agree that these approaches for managing information are inefficient and error-prone.

Databases were developed out of a need for efficient and reliable handling of information.

What is a database?

A database is a system that enables users to use, manage, and share data. An organized mechanism can be used to store, access, and retrieve data effectively.

In order to create, use, and manage a database, you will have to understand a few things about them:

- Databases are meant to be used by a large number of users. It should be designed to allow them to conveniently perform actions such as adding, inserting, modifying, or retrieving data.
- A hard drive crash or system failure can cause loss of important information. A database system requires mechanisms to enable recovery from these failures.
- The use of databases poses risks such as accidental overwriting of data and information theft. Hence, when designing databases, you will have to consider the security aspects.

Relational Database

Relational databases are based on the relational model for database management proposed by Edgar F. Codd, a computer scientist in the 1970s. A relational database allows users to identify, store, access, and retrieve related data. In a relational database, data is organized by tables, which may contain multiple records and columns.

A database is an organized mechanism that you can use to store, manipulate, and retrieve data. A simple example of a database is your phone directory. A telephone directory commonly contains information such as people's name, address, and phone number. The entries are usually presented in alphabetical order which makes searching easier.

Dr. Edgar F. Codd proposed the concept of relational databases while he was working as a researcher at IBM. IBM released System R which was based on his database model. However, it was the Oracle Corporation that promoted the first SQL, which was aptly called the ORACLE database.

Relational Database Management Systems (RDBMS) allows organizations such as businesses to efficiently and effectively manage complex and enormous amounts of data. SQL is the most popular language to access relational databases and through the years, multiple implementations of SQL were developed to respond to the varying and growing needs of users for data management. Although the various SQL versions generally adhere to the fundamental SQL standards, they admittedly come in varying flavors and nuances.

At present, the following are the most widely used RDBMS:

- MySQL

MySQL supports multiple platforms such as MS Windows, UNIX, and Mac OS X. It offers an open source version as well as a commercial one. MySQL works well with web engines and it is commonly used with PHP in web development. Oracle Corporation now owns MySQL.

- PostgreSQL

PostgreSQL is a general purpose extensible RDBMS. It supports custom functions created through various computer languages such as Java and C/C++. It is reliable, free, and easy to use.

- Db2

DB2 is an easy to use and stable RDBMS that can work well with Oracle's SQL.

- SQLite

SQLite is an open source SQL database system. It is capable of storing a database in a single file. It is commonly used for databases in portable gadgets such as smartphones, MP3 players, and PDAs.

- MS SQL Server

MS SQL Server is a commercial database system developed by Microsoft. It only offers support for the Windows OS. It uses ANSI SQL and T-SQL as its main query languages.

- Oracle DB

Oracle DB is a commercial database owned by Oracle Corporation. It offers integrated business solutions for managing complex database needs of large organizations.

- MS Access

MS Access is a Microsoft Office product that can be used to handle simple database functions. It supports importation of data from different sources. It allows users to write queries easily without having to memorize syntax.

BASIC SQL VOCABULARY

Now that you have a good idea of what database is about, it is time to get to know the terms that you will be using as you learn SQL

Schema

A schema is the set of database objects associated to a database user. Each username is linked to one schema. A user manages the database objects associated to his/her username. Subject to the schemes of permissions granted by the database administrator, a user can create, remove, or manipulate data objects linked to him/her.

Table

Tables are the primary data storage tool for databases. A relational database system commonly uses multiple tables to store data. A table is formed by a set of elements arranged in columns and rows.

The following is an example of a table:

ID	FIRSTNAME	LASTNAME	JOBTITLE	DEPARTMENT	MONTHLYPAY
190005	John	Watson	Dispatcher	Administration	5000.00
190006	Mickey	Malone	Officer	Operations	7000.00
190007	Kirsten	Dunk	Manager	Administration	8000.00
190008	Chinkee	Stuart	Agent	Sales	6000.00
190009	Sherry	Lynx	Executive	Management	10000.00

The EMPLOYEES table has 6 columns: ID, FIRSTNAME, LASTNAME, JOBTITLE, DEPARTMENT, and MONTHLYPAY.

The rows are related data, which are arranged horizontally.

The number of columns used by a table is limited by the table definition while the number of rows can be unlimited.

Column

Columns are defined and identified through their column name, data type, and other attributes. A database table contains at least one column.

The column names in the above table are ID, FIRSTNAME, LASTNAME, JOBTITLE, DEPARTMENT, and MONTHLY PAY. These columns are further defined by the data type and other attributes for each column.

Below are the column names of the EMPLOYEES table:

```
+----------+------------+----------+----------+------------------+------------+
| ID       | FIRSTNAME  | LASTNAME | JOBTITLE | DEPARTMENT       | MONTHLYPAY |
+----------+------------+----------+----------+------------------+------------+
```

Record

A record is the row of related data in a table. The rows hold the records for each column.

For example, a record or row in the EMPLOYEES table consists of related information about each employee such as his or her ID, first name, last name, job title, department, and salary.

Below is the first record in the EMPLOYEES database:

```
| 190005 | John     | Watson   | Dispatcher | Administration |    5000.00 |
```

Field

A field, also known as cell, is the intersection point of a column and a row. A table contains at least one cell. If a table has 6 columns and 6 rows, we can say that it has 36 fields.

The following snippet of the EMPLOYEES table shows the column names and a row of data. An example of a cell would be the space that contains the data 'John' under the FIRSTNAME column. Another example would be the integer 190005 stored under the ID column.

```
+--------+-----------+----------+-----------+----------------+-----------+
| ID     | FIRSTNAME | LASTNAME | JOBTITLE  | DEPARTMENT     | MONTHLYPAY |
+--------+-----------+----------+-----------+----------------+-----------+
| 190005 | John      | Watson   | Dispatcher | Administration |  5000.00  |
```

SQL Syntax

SQL syntax refers to the rules and conventions that specify how SQL codes should be written and interpreted. SQL uses simple syntax and its statements are almost like your regular English phrases.

SQL Statements

An SQL statement consists of a series of keywords, identifiers, parameters, and other values that ends in a semicolon (;). The semicolon can also serve as a statement separator in cases where the database system allows users to execute multiple commands in a single call.

Following are examples of SQL statements:

CREATE DATABASE xyzcompany;

CREATE TABLE my_table;

INSERT INTO EMPLOYEES
VALUES (190010, 'James', 'Newman', 'Sales', 3500.00);

An SQL statement consists of the following parts:

Clause

Clauses are commands that indicate the action or task to be performed. By convention, clauses are written in uppercase letters.

Examples:

CREATE TABLE
INSERT INTO

Table name

The table specified in an SQL statement is the recipient of the database action.

Parameter

The parameters refer to the columns, data types, and values passed as argument.

SQL statements have flexible structures. You may write a statement in a single line or spread a statement across several lines.

Case Sensitivity

SQL is not a case-sensitive language. You may opt to write a keyword in uppercase or lowercase as you wish. You can name a database or table in uppercase and access the same in lowercase. For example, you can create a table named "STUDENTS" and access the table in queries as "students."

However, do keep in mind that database engines are case-sensitive when it comes to data. If you saved data in a certain case and access the same in a different case, the database engine will interpret the query as a different object and raise an error.

By convention, programmers write the commands in uppercase. For universality, it is better to stick to this convention.
□

SQL Comments

An SQL comment is a language feature than can be used to provide additional information about an SQL statement or process. It is a text that will be ignored by the database engine.

In SQL, you can write comments in a single line or in multiple lines. There are slight differences in writing single-line and multi-line comments.

Single-line comments starts with two hyphens (--).

Example:

```
-- Select all members
SELECT * FROM members
```

Multi-line comments are set off with a combination of slash and asterisk (/*) and end with a combination of asterisk and slash (*/).

Example:

```
/* Select all the members whose
age is greater than 18 */
SELECT * FROM Employees
WHERE age > 18;
```

Summary:

A database is an organized mechanism for storing, accessing, managing, retrieving, and sharing data. Relational databases are based on the relational model for database management proposed by Edgar F. Codd. In relational databases, data is organized into tables that may contain several rows and columns. SQL implements simple and flexible syntax. It is a case-insensitive language.

Chapter 3: SQL Data Types

The data type attribute specifies the type of information that will be stored on a database table. You will be using this attribute to design tables that will work seamlessly together to provide accurate, relevant, and functional data on a timely manner.

The data type is an important attribute in databases because it also defines the type of operations that users can perform on a table and consequently, on a database.

Data types may vary slightly with each SQL implementation. In order to effectively and properly manage and run your database system, you will have to indentify and learn the specific data types supported by your SQL version.

SQL data types can be broadly categorized into character, number, date and time, and Boolean data.

The major SQL versions generally support the following categories of data types:

Character String
Unicode Character Strings

Exact Numeric Data

Approximate Numeric

Time and Date Data

Boolean Data

Binary Data

Character String

The string data type includes CHAR, VARCHAR, and TEXT.

CHAR ()

The CHAR string type consists of a fixed length non-Unicode character. It accepts an argument for the number of characters it would store. The actual data entered is space-padded on the right to match the table definition for size. The string type has a maximum size of 8,000 characters.

VARCHAR ()

The VARCHAR data type is a non-binary string. Its values are not space padded. It is saved and displayed in the same format.

It takes an argument for the number of characters it would store. The VARCHAR string type can have a varying size of up to 8,000 characters.

TEXT

The TEXT data type represents non-binary strings of varying sizes. It can hold a maximum of 2,147,483,647 characters.

The following character types are variants of the TEXT type:

LONGTEXT	4,294,967,295 characters
MEDIUMTEXT	16,777,215 characters
TINYTEXT	255 characters

Unicode Character String

nchar

The nchar data type can have a maximum size of 4,000 characters.

Nvarchar

The nvarchar is Unicode data type with variable size of up to 4,000 characters.

ntext

The ntext is a Unicode data type with a variable size of up to 1,073,741,823 characters.

Binary Data Types

BINARY
Binary is a binary data type with a fixed size of up to 8,000 bytes.

VARBINARY
Varbinary is a binary data type with variable size of up to 8,000 bytes.

VARBINARY (max)
Barbinary(max) is a binary data type with a maximum size of 231 bytes.

image

Image is a binary data type with a variable length of up to 2,147,483,647 bytes.

BLOB

BLOB stands for Binary Large Object, a data type that can contain large amounts of files, data, or documents.

Below are the types of BLOB and the maximum size for each type:

BLOB	65,535 bytes
LONGBLOB	4,294,967,295 characters
MEDIUMBLOB	16,777,215 characters
TINYBLOB	255 characters

Numeric Data Types

All numeric data types have a precision value.

The precision value specifies the total significant digits of a number. In addition, numeric data types have an optional scale value that indicates the number of decimal places to the right side of the decimal point.

For example, the number 2129546.32 has a precision of 9 with a scale of 2. If you are going to declare this number in a statement, you will define it as DECIMAL(9,2);

Exact Numeric Data Types

SQL supports exact numeric data types such as Integer and SMALLINT as well as some extension integer types.

DECIMAL

The DECIMAL numeric data type is a fixed-point type that you can use to work with exact numeric values.

For example, the statement DECIMAL(5,2) defines a column with a precision of 5 and scale of 2. This indicates that a column will store numeric data with 5 digits and 2 decimal numbers. The default value for a DECIMAL data type is 10. When no value or zero value is assigned to scale, it indicates that the number has no fractional part or decimal numbers.

A decimal data type can have a maximum of 65 digits.

Approximate Numeric Types

SQL supports the following approximate numeric types:

REAL Number

A real number uses binary precision.

FLOAT

A float uses binary precision when rounding.
Usage: FLOAT(precision)

DOUBLE PRECISION

Double precision is an approximate numeric type, which uses binary precision. Its default precision must be higher than the precision assigned to the REAL number.

Usage: DOUBLE PRECISION

Time and Date Data Types

This category includes the following data types:

DATE
TIME
DATETIME
YEAR
TIMESTAMP

DATE

The DATE data type stores the year, month, and day. It is displayed as YYYY-MM-DD. The date type can range from 1000-01-01 to 9999-12-31. It is commonly used when only the date is required and not the time.

TIME

The TIME data type contains the hour, minute, and seconds values.

DATETIME

The DATETIME type is displayed as YYYY-MM-DD HH:MM:SS. Its value ranges from 1000-01-01 00:00:00 to 9999-12-31 23:59:59. This data type is used when both date and time data are required.

YEAR

The YEAR data type stores year values. Its syntax is YEAR() and you can pass an argument of either 4 or 2 to display the year in four (YYYY) or two (YY) characters, respectively. When the YEAR is displayed in a four-digit format, values range from 1901 to 2155. When it is displayed in a two-digit format, only the last two digits are returned.

TIMESTAMP

The TIMESTAMP data type is a temporal data type, which is used to store the combination of date and time. It is displayed in

33

the format YYYY-MM-DD-HH:MM:SS and it is fixed at 19 characters.

Summary

The data type attribute is used to specify the type of information that will be recorded on a table. The data type also defines the type of operations that users can perform on the different columns of a table. SQL supports several data types including character string, numeric, binary, exact numeric type, approximate numeric type, date and time data type, and Boolean data.

Chapter 4: SQL Commands

In this chapter, you will have an overview of the standard commands that you can use to interact with databases. These commands are commonly grouped based on their nature or function. There are at least six categories of commands in SQL. You will be learning more about them on succeeding chapters.

Data Definition Language (DDL)

DDL statements allow you to set up, modify, arrange, and remove database objects such as tables, views, and indices. This set of commands lets you work efficiently with databases on a fundamental level. You will be using these commands frequently to design or drop database objects as needed.

These statements include the following:

CREATE TABLE
CREATE INDEX
CREATE VIEW

ALTER TABLE

ALTER INDEX

DROP TABLE

DROP INDEX

DROP VIEW

Data Manipulation Language (DML)

This SQL aspect lets you modify information in database objects. The DML statements facilitate flexibility in data handling and maintenance by allowing users to update information, introduce new data, and delete objects when necessary.

The DML commands include the following:

UPDATE

INSERT

DELETE

Data Query Language (DQL)

The DQL statements are used to retrieve information from relational databases. The primary DQL command is:

SELECT

The "SELECT" statement lets you add clauses and options to refine queries and enable users to obtain the desired information from the most complex relational database systems. Many consider DQL as the most powerful aspect of SQL.

Data Control Language (DCL)

DCL statements are used to manage database access rights. These commands are commonly used to generate database objects related to access rights. They allow administrators to assign and terminate access privileges as well as modify passwords. Databases are often used to store sensitive information, including clients' personal and credit card information. The proper and timely use of DCL commands helps protect the security and integrity of these data.

Here are the most frequently used DCL commands:

REVOKE
GRANT
ALTER PASSWORD
CREATE SYNONYM

Data Administration Commands

These commands let you perform audits and analyze operations within the database. You can also use them to assess the system's performance.

The data administration commands include the following:

START AUDIT
STOP AUDIT

Take note that data administration is not the same as database administration. Database administration refers to the overall management of databases and involves the use of all commands. It is more specific to individual SQL implementations.

Transactional Data Commands

This set of commands is used to manage transactions within the database.

SET TRANSACTION: This command is used to assign names and attributes to database transactions.

COMMIT: The COMMIT command is used to save database transactions.

SAVEPOINT: This command is used to create points within transaction groups. You will need this to execute a ROLLBACK.

ROLLBACK: The ROLLBACK statement is used to undo transactions.

Summary:

SQL offers six main categories of commands based on functionality: Data Definition Language (DDL), Data Manipulation Language (DML), Data Query Language (DQL),

Data Control Language (DCL), Data Administration Commands, and Transactional Data Commands.

Chapter 5: Designing and Creating Databases

A database is a collection of related data. It is organized to enable easy access and efficient data management. When correctly designed, it can provide relevant, updated, and accurate information to its users. Investing time on the design of a database makes sense because you would want it to satisfy your needs and at the same time, be flexible enough to accommodate future changes.

Designing the Database

There are two underlying principles of database design that you should keep in mind:

First, redundant or duplicate data should be avoided because they waste premium space and make your database susceptible to inconsistencies and errors.

Second, the completeness and accuracy of information in a database is paramount. A database with inaccurate information will produce inaccurate reports. Users who rely on these flawed reports for their decision making process will end up with misinformed or erroneous judgment.

A properly designed database has the following attributes:

- It organizes data into subject-oriented tables to minimize duplicate information.
- It provides the database system with the information needed to combine data from multiple tables as required.
- It accommodates the users' requirements for data processing and reporting.
- It helps enforce data integrity and accuracy.

Designing a database is a multi-step process. Below are the steps you have to consider when creating a database:

1. Identify the purpose of the database.

This initial step involves identifying the objectives, usage, and users of the database. It is like writing down a mission statement that you can refer to in the course of designing the database.

For small businesses with simple databases, it could be written in a short statement like this:

"The database stores client data for the purpose of generating reports and mailing information."

For bigger businesses with complex databases, it could very well take up a paragraph or page.

2. Gather and organize the data needed.

Collect all kinds of data that you think should be included in the database. These may include details such as product codes, item names, department names, invoice numbers, and addresses. Identify the types of reports or outputs required and create a prototype for each.

Break every piece of data down to its smallest usable or logical portion. Names, for example, are typically broken down into two pieces of data: the first name and last name. This practice facilitates the sorting of last names alphabetically. If an information item needs to be sorted, searched, calculated, and reported on, that item should be in a field.

Visualizing the questions that the database might have to answer can help you uncover more items to include in the database.

3. Segregate the data by subjects and assign each subject to a table.

Categorize the information by topic and design a table for each topic. Choose the major subjects and create a table out of them. For example, after collecting and organizing data, you might come up with this initial list:

Products
Product ID
Product Name
Price
Units in Stock
Units on Order

Suppliers
Supplier ID
Company Name
Contact Person:
Contact Number
Address
City, State, Zip

Orders
Order Number
Order Date
Product ID
Product
Quantity
Price

Customers
ID
Name
Title
Address
City, State, ZIP
Contact Number
E-mail Address

The major subjects indicated by the list are the products, sales orders, suppliers, and customers. It would be a practical idea to start with four tables based on this list. You can add to the list later as you work on the design.

Notice how the information items are separated into simple sets where there are no redundant data. Having the information in their proper place enables users to easily and efficiently modify information. A well-designed database should not contain duplicate data. If you have to repeat the information in several lists, you will have to create another table to handle that item.

4. Convert data headings into columns.

Determine the type of data each table should have. Every item in the table constitutes a field, which is shown as a column. A Sales table, for example, might contain fields such as Quantity or Unit Price. The field information can be used as column headings for the table.

After identifying the preliminary list of columns for your table, you can start refining them to make the data more responsive to your reporting needs. For instance, splitting the customer names into two columns will allow you to search, index, and sort on the specific column. Likewise, it would be a good practice to put the address components into separate columns to allow searching, filtering, or sorting operations on each component. You may want, for example, to sort the customers based on their state or city.

Here is a practical tip when setting up the columns: Avoid including calculated data unless it is necessarily and otherwise unavailable. They not only unnecessarily clog the database; they may become obsolete and useless in time. Instead, have SQL perform the calculations for you, as you need them.

5. Define the primary key.

A table should have at least one primary key, which will be used to provide a unique identification for every record in the table. A primary key could be the Employee ID, Item Code, Product ID or other data that are uniquely identified to an item or data.

SQL uses the primary key fields to rapidly search for, collect, and display related data across several tables.

If your table already contains a unique value that will always be different from other records, it would be practical to assign that field as the primary key. A primary key should always be a unique identifier. Using people's names as primary key is not a good idea because there could easily be two people with identical names in a list.

When selecting the primary key, do choose a field that will always require a value. Fields that allow unknown, unassigned, or null values now and at some future time should not be specified as the primary key.

A primary key's value should be unchanging. In relational databases, the primary key is typically referenced by multiple tables. A change in the value of the primary key must be implemented in all tables that are using the key as a reference. Selecting a primary key with a fixed value will help lessen the possibility of invalid referencing within the database.

In some cases, it may not be as easy to identify a good field for a primary key. You might want to consider including a column with Auto Increment numeric data type for use as the table's primary key. This identifier is ideal for use as the primary key because its values are fixed and unique for each row. In addition, the values are not associated with factual data that the rows represent. Hence, any changes in information about the row will have no impact on the primary key values.

You may also find it more suitable to designate two or more columns as the primary key. Composite keys use at least two columns. In the Order list shown above, the table could be made more efficient and useful by designating both Product ID and ORDER Number as the primary keys.

6. Establish relationships between tables.

Examine all tables and determine the association between the data stored in them. If you have to, add columns or create more tables to refine the relationships.

Earlier, you have broken the data down to their most basic level. This time, you will have to find meaningful ways to bring them together.

One-to-Many Relationship

In the real world, a supplier normally provides more than one product to their customers. Hence, if you will represent a supplier in a Suppliers table, there will be multiple products associated to that supplier in the Products table. The relationship between the two tables is known as one-to-many.

Analyze the following diagram:

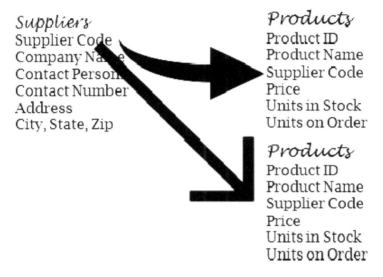

The above figure represents the relationship between the Suppliers and Products table. Notice that the Supplier Code, which is the primary key of Supplier's table and is one of the fields in the Products table, connects the Supplier's table to the Products table.

That is how you will represent the one-to-many relationship in your database. Identify the primary key of the "one" side and include that as one of the columns on the other side. For instance, in the above illustration, if you want to know the right supplier for a product, you can use the Supplier Code in the Products table to fetch the name and other information you may want to know about the supplier.

The Supplier Code is the primary key of the Supplier's table. On the side of the Products table, the Supplier Code column is a foreign key. It is a foreign key because it is a primary key of another table, the Suppliers table.

Many-to-Many Relationship

The many-to-many relationship is illustrated by the relationship between the Orders Table and the Products table.

On one side, an order can have multiple products. On the other side, a product can have several orders. Applying this relationship to a database, it means that a record in the Orders table may correspond to multiple records in the Products table and vice versa.

Obviously, you cannot apply the same solution you have used to capture the one-to-many relationship. For example, if you try to link the two tables through the Product Code, you may have to prepare multiple orders for a single transaction to reflect each product listed in the Order. That could result to inefficiency and erroneous data.

What is the best way to reflect this type of relationship in your database?

Solution: Create a new table.

This new table can be used to simplify a many-to-many relationship to a one-to-many relationship. The trick is to add the primary keys of the pair of tables into the new table, which is more popularly known as junction table. This table will be used to record all occurrences of the relationship.

One-to-One Relationship

A one-to-one relationship could occur in instances where you have to handle supplementary information that does not apply to most items and are only occasionally required. This type of information is commonly handled in a different table. In such cases, the main table and the supplemental table should have a common field.

There are at least two ways to represent the one-to-one relationship in the database.

If the tables have similar topic, you may consider establishing the relationship by specifying the same primary key.

If they have different topic and primary key, you can assign the primary key of one table as a foreign key on the other table.

7. Analyze and improve the database design.

Scrutinize the design to spot possible errors. Construct the tables and do a dry run by encoding test data. Analyze if the tables can produce the information you need. Make adjustments if you have to.

After constructing the tables and establishing the relationships between them, you can start populating them with test data. You should try performing regular transactions like appending new records, creating queries, and updating data. Simulating typical transactions at this time will help you identify possible issues.
You have to check if the database is capable of providing the data you want and need. Look out for data redundancy and modify the database design to eliminate inconsistencies and inefficiencies.

In the process, you might find areas that need improvement. You can use the following guide to identify flaws in the database design:

Check for columns that can be calculated from existing columns. You can make your database more efficient by weeding out unnecessary columns and data.

Check the database for any missing information that should have been included. Verify if the current tables can accommodate it. If not, decide if you have to make a new table for it. Remember that a column is usually required for any information that you may need particularly if it cannot be produced by performing calculations on existing columns.

Analyze each table and see if all columns provide information about the subject of the table. Otherwise, these columns should be placed in a separate table.

If you find yourself repeatedly encoding the same information in one table, you may need to split them and link their data by creating a one-to-many relationship between the old and the new table.

If one or more tables end up with too many columns, too few rows, and many empty fields, you may need to redesign them so they can have more rows and fewer columns.

Review the tables and determine if all relationships between them are represented. Bear in mind that you need to provide at least one common column to capture one-to-many and one-to-one relationships and a third table to reflect the many-to-many relationships between two tables.

Evaluate the tables and ascertain if all pieces of data are in their smallest logical form. A piece of information that has to be sorted, searched, calculated on, and reported should be placed in a column.

8. Implement normalization rules.

Check if your tables are structured properly by applying data normalization rules.

Database normalization is the technique of organizing data into tables based on a series of forms. The process involves the successive application of rules to help ensure that items of data are placed into appropriate tables and that each table is assigned to a specific topic. The rules are applied to help you decide if your tables are structured properly.

Normalizing a database helps eliminate duplicate data, avoid data modification issues, and simplify query.

The rules are applied sequentially as your database design is evaluated through a series of normal forms. This means that a table must first comply with the first form before it can proceed to the second form and so on. There are five generally accepted normal forms but most designs require only the first three forms.

First Normal Form

A table should comply with the following rules in order to be in the First Normal Form:

- Each field should contain only one value.
- A column should contain only one type of value.
- All columns should have unique names.

Second Normal Form

A table should adhere to the following rules to be in the Second Normal Form:

- A table must have satisfied the requirements for the First Normal Form.
- All non-primary key columns must be dependent on the complete primary key. The rule seeks to eliminate partial dependency, which is usually an issue when the table uses a composite key or more than one primary key. It stresses direct dependence on the primary key and rules out indirect dependence through attributes.

Third Normal Form

A table must satisfy the following rules to be in the Third Normal Form:

- It must have complied with the requirements of the Second Normal Form.
- All non-key columns must be independent of each other.

If a table stores non-key values that change when another value changes, then that table is violating the rules of the Third Normal Form. Hence, to be compliant with this form, a table could not store derived information that depends on another value.

Creating a Database

Once you have finalized your database design, you will be ready to tackle the procedural side of working with databases.

Before you can start creating your table, you have to create the database that will store all tables and data. Make sure that your database is stored in a secure location and that your hardware is well maintained.

Creating a database is a straightforward operation. You will use this syntax:

CREATE DATABASE database_name;

For example, let us say you want to create a database and you want to name it phoenixcompany, you can use this statement:

CREATE DATABASE phoenixcompany;

The above statement creates the phoenixcompany database. At this point, you have a database on standby. Before you can start using it, you have to designate it as the active database. To do this, run the USE command with the database name to activate or specify the default database.

For example, to specify the phoenixcompany as the active database, you will execute this statement:

USE phoenixcompany;

Whenever you start a session in MySQL, you need to run the USE command to access the database you want to work on. If you need to work with multiple files, you can shift between databases with the USE command.

Take note that you cannot have duplicate database names in the same server. To ensure that the name you will be giving to a database is unique, you can use the IF NOT EXISTS clause when you run the CREATE DATABASE command:

CREATE DATABASE IF NOT EXISTS phoenixcompany;

You can also view the databases stored on the server by executing this statement:

SHOW DATABASE;

Removing a Database

You can remove a database as easily as you have created it. The DROP command is used to remove a database.

Syntax:

DROP DATABASE database_name

The DROP command is an extremely powerful command that can cause massive loss of data when executed improperly. Dropping a database will typically require admin privileges.

Summary

Database is a collection of related data. There are two underlying principles in database design: 1. Redundant or duplicate data should be avoided. 2. Completeness and accuracy of data is essential.

Database design is a multi-step process consisting of the following steps:

1. Identify the purpose of the database.
2. Gather and organized the required data.
3. Sort the data based on subjects and assign each subject to a table.
4. Convert data headings into columns.
5. Define the primary key.
6. Establish relationships between tables.
7. Review and improve the database design.
8. Implement normalization rules.

Chapter 6: Creating Tables & Populating Tables with Data

Tables are the main storage of information in a database. A database has at least one table. Complex databases contain multiple tables that are related to each other.

In Chapter 5, you have learned the important principles of database design. You can use those concepts to design, plan, and create tables that will store every bit of information you need to work on.

In this chapter, you will learn the SQL commands to create tables and populate them with data.

Creating Tables

In SQL, creating a table involves declaring a table name, defining its columns, and specifying each column's data type.

When you invest time to design your database properly, you will find that it is so much easier to do the procedural tasks of running the commands to create the tables.

Before you start creating tables, here are questions that you can use as a guide for designing, constructing, and naming your table.

What is the most appropriate identifier for this table?
What headings should I use for each column?
What data types will I be working with?
Which column(s) can be used as the main key(s) for the table?
What type of data should be assigned to each column?
What is the maximum width for each column?
Which columns could be empty and which could not be empty?

It is a sound practice to name your table based on its subject. For example, if your table is all about products, you may name it as Products. If it will hold data about employees, you might as well name it EMPLOYEES.

The column titles normally describe the data that will be recorded on the column. You may use abbreviations but it is always better to use one, which is readable and easily recognizable.

Every table in a relational database should have a primary key to be useful in queries. You have to choose a column with values that will not change over time and this column has to be declared as a NOT NULL column.

When determining the maximum width for your column, consider the normal range or length of data that will be stored for each column and work around that figure.

To create a new table, you can either start from ground zero or use the structure and definition of an existing table.

Creating a New Table From Scratch

The keyword CREATE TABLE is used to define a new table. Just after this clause and on the same line, you will have to specify a unique identifier. This statement is followed by a block of statements specifying the column name, the data type that you want to store in each column, and other attributes you may want to add.

Syntax:

```
CREATE TABLE table_name
(
    column1 datatype [NULL|NOT NULL]
    column2 datatype [NULL|NOT NULL]
    ...
);
```

The table_name stands for the table's identifier.

The parameters column1 and column2 are the identifiers for the columns that you want the table to have. Each column should be assigned a data type. It is defined as either NULL or NOT NULL. If you do not specify this attribute, the default attribute is NULL.

The example below will demonstrate table creation commands. This table will be saved in the phoenixcompany database and it will be named EMPLOYEES:

```
CREATE TABLE EMPLOYEES(
ID INT(6) NOT NULL,
FIRSTNAME VARCHAR(20) NOT NULL,
LASTNAME VARCHAR(20) NOT NULL,
JOBTITLE VARCHAR (30),
DEPARTMENT VARCHAR(15),
MONTHLYPAY DECIMAL(9,2),
```

PRIMARY KEY (ID)
);

The above statements will create a table with 6 columns.

The first column, ID field, was designated in the last statement as the table's primary key. It will store each employee's unique identification number. It was specified as an integer data type with a precision of 6. It will not accept a NULL value.

The second column, FIRSTNAME was specified as a VARCHAR type with a maximum size of 20 characters. The FIRSTNAME column will store the first name of each employee.

The third column, LASTNAME, is a VARCHAR data type with a maximum size of 20 characters. This column will hold the last name of each employee.

The fourth column, JOBTITLE, is a VARCHAR data type with a maximum of 30 characters. This column will store each employee's job title.

The fifth column, DEPARTMENT, is a VARCHAR data type with a maximum of 15 characters. This column will be used to store each employee's department.

The sixth column, MONTHLYPAY, is a DECIMAL data type with a precision of 9 and scale of 2. It will store each employee's monthly salary.

You can see the table structure by writing the DESC statement with the table name.

For example, to view the structure of the EMPLOYEES table, you can write this statement;

DESC EMPLOYEES;

Output:

```
+-------------+--------------+------+-----+---------+-------+
| Field       | Type         | Null | Key | Default | Extra |
+-------------+--------------+------+-----+---------+-------+
| ID          | int(6)       | NO   | PRI | NULL    |       |
| FIRSTNAME   | varchar(20)  | NO   |     | NULL    |       |
| LASTNAME    | varchar(20)  | NO   |     | NULL    |       |
| JOBTITLE    | varchar(30)  | YES  |     | NULL    |       |
| DEPARTMENT  | varchar(15)  | YES  |     | NULL    |       |
| MONTHLYPAY  | decimal(9,2) | YES  |     | NULL    |       |
+-------------+--------------+------+-----+---------+-------+
6 rows in set (0.07 sec)
```

Creating a New Table from Existing Tables

You can also create a new table based on the structures of an existing table by combining the command CREATE TABLE with the SELECT and FROM keywords.

Here is the syntax:

```
CREATE TABLE new_table name AS
(
    SELECT [column1, column 2...column...]
    FROM existing_table_name
    [WHERE]
);
```

Executing the code will create a new table with the same column definitions as the existing table specified by the FROM command. The SELECT command allows you to choose the columns that you want to include in the new table. The command will also import data from the original table. This feature makes database operations more efficient by considerably reducing the time it takes to set up and/or populate a new table.

To see how it works, you can create a duplicate table named INVESTORS from the existing table EMPLOYEES that you have created earlier. You will copy the entire column definitions of the original table using these statements:

CREATE TABLE INVESTORS AS
SELECT ID, FIRSTNAME, LASTNAME, JOBTITLE, DEPARTMENT, MONTHLYPAY
FROM EMPLOYEES;

The above command will create the table INVESTORS with the same column names and definitions as the table EMPLOYEES.

Populating a Table

Now that you have set up the tables for your database, you are ready to start making them useful by adding data. SQL's Data Manipulate Language enables users to perform changes to databases. You can use this set of commands to fill a table with data, update the table, and eliminate unnecessary information.

Populating a Table with New Data

To add new data to a table, you can either enter them manually or execute automated entry using an application.

Manually populating table involves data entry through a keyboard. Automated data entry, on the other hand, involves loading data from an external source using a computer program. It includes data transfer from one database to another.

While you have learned that SQL keywords are case insensitive, this is not true with data. You have to practice consistency when entering data and executing data queries to ensure that there will be no issues when using them in various operations. For example, if you store an employee's name as 'Archer', future references to this piece of data should always be 'Archer'. If you specify 'archer' or 'ARCHER', this will be processed as a different data and it will return an error if there is no existing data with the same name.

For data uniformity, it is a good practice to write a style guide for your data. This is important specially if you have multiple users.

Adding Records Using the INSERT command

The INSERT command is used to add a record to a table. Invoking the INSERT command will insert a new row of data to a table.

You can use the INSERT command either to add data to all columns or to add selected columns to a table.

If your objective is to add records to all columns, you will have to use the INSERT command with the VALUES keyword to specify the values for the columns. These statements will assign the VALUES parameters sequentially to the table's columns.

Below is the syntax for this format:

```
INSERT INTO table_name
VALUES ('value1', 'value2'... [NULL];
```

However, if you only need to update selected columns, you will have to specify the column names. The values will be assigned based about the columns you have specified.

Here is the syntax:

```
INSERT INTO table_name (column1, column2, column3)
VALUES ('value1', 'value2', 'value3');
```

You will notice that a comma is used to separate the column names and the values. If your values include literal string and date or time data, you will need to enclose them in quotation marks.

To demonstrate the insert operation, let us say that you have the following record for one employee:

ID   190005
First Name   John
Last Name   Watson
Job Title   Dispatcher
Department   Administration
Monthly Pay   5,000.00

To add all the above information into the EMPLOYEES table, you will use these statements:

INSERT INTO EMPLOYEES (ID, FIRSTNAME, LASTNAME, JOBTITLE, MONTHLYPAYS)
VALUES (190005, 'John', 'Watson', 'Dispatcher', 'Administration', 5000.00);

To view the updated table, you can use this syntax:

SELECT * FROM table_name;

The wildcard (*) is used to specify all fields on the table.

To display all data stored in the EMPLOYEES' table, you can execute this statement:

SELECT * FROM EMPLOYEES

Here is a screenshot of the result:

```
+---------+-----------+----------+------------+----------------+------------+
| ID      | FIRSTNAME | LASTNAME | JOBTITLE   | DEPARTMENT     | MONTHLYPAY |
+---------+-----------+----------+------------+----------------+------------+
| 190005  | John      | Watson   | Dispatcher | Administration |    5000.00 |
+---------+-----------+----------+------------+----------------+------------+
1 row in set (0.00 sec)
```

Assuming you only want to view the first name, last name and the job title of the employee, you can execute this statement:

SELECT FIRSTNAME, LASTNAME, JOBTITLE FROM EMPLOYEES;

Here is the result:

```
+-----------+----------+------------+
| FIRSTNAME | LASTNAME | JOBTITLE   |
+-----------+----------+------------+
| John      | Watson   | Dispatcher |
+-----------+----------+------------+
1 row in set (0.00 sec)
```

You can try to populate the table further with the following information:

73

ID NO.	FIRST NAME	LAST NAME	JOB TITLE	DEPARTMENT	MONTHLY PAY
190006	Mickey	Malone	Officer	Operations	7,000.00
190007	Kirsten	Dunk	Manager	Administration	8,000.00
190008	Chinkee	Stuart	Agent	Sales	6,000.00

You will have to use the INSERT INTO command for each record that you want to add to the table. Here is how you will normally write the statements:

INSERT INTO EMPLOYEES
VALUES(190006, 'Mickey', 'Malone', 'Officer', 'Operations', 7000.00);

INSERT INTO EMPLOYEES
VALUES(190007'Kirsten', 'Dunk', 'Manager', 'Administration', 8000.00);

INSERT INTO EMPLOYEES
VALUES(190008, 'Chinkee', 'Stuart', 'Agent', 'Sales', 6000.00);

To fetch all data stored in the EMPLOYEES table, use the SELECT command with the wild card character:

SELECT * EMPLOYEES

Here is a screenshot of the updated table:

```
+--------+-----------+----------+------------+----------------+------------+
| ID     | FIRSTNAME | LASTNAME | JOBTITLE   | DEPARTMENT     | MONTHLYPAY |
+--------+-----------+----------+------------+----------------+------------+
| 190005 | John      | Watson   | Dispatcher | Administration |    5000.00 |
| 190006 | Mickey    | Malone   | Officer    | Operations     |    7000.00 |
| 190007 | Kirsten   | Dunk     | Manager    | Administration |    8000.00 |
| 190008 | Chinkee   | Stuart   | Agent      | Sales          |    6000.00 |
+--------+-----------+----------+------------+----------------+------------+
4 rows in set (0.00 sec)
```

You can also insert data to specific columns by specifying the column name and assigning their corresponding values as VALUES parameters. For example, if you only have the employee number, first name, last name, and job title, you will have to specify the column names first as parameters.

To see how this works, you can try adding the following data to the EMPLOYEES table:

ID NO.	FIRST NAME	LAST NAME	JOB TITLE	DEPARTMENT	MONTHLY PAY
190009	Sherry	Lynx	Executive		

You can add the above data to the EMPLOYEES table with the following statements:

INSERT INTO EMPLOYEES (ID, FIRSTNAME, LASTNAME, JOBTITLE)
VALUES (190009, 'Sherry", 'Lynx', 'Executive');

Here is the screenshot of the updated EMPLOYEES table:

```
+--------+-----------+----------+-----------+----------------+------------+
| ID     | FIRSTNAME | LASTNAME | JOBTITLE  | DEPARTMENT     | MONTHLYPAY |
+--------+-----------+----------+-----------+----------------+------------+
| 190005 | John      | Watson   | Dispatcher| Administration |    5000.00 |
| 190006 | Mickey    | Malone   | Officer   | Operations     |    7000.00 |
| 190007 | Kirsten   | Dunk     | Manager   | Administration |    8000.00 |
| 190008 | Chinkee   | Stuart   | Agent     | Sales          |    6000.00 |
| 190009 | Sherry    | Lynx     | Executive | NULL           |       NULL |
+--------+-----------+----------+-----------+----------------+------------+
5 rows in set (0.00 sec)
```

Take note that the default value 'NULL' was displayed for the empty records.

Inserting NULL Values

The 'NULL' value is not always a default value. You may also insert 'NULL' values to a table.

For example, you can provide NULL values in place of empty data with this statement:

INSERT INTO EMPLOYEES

VALUES (190010, 'Julie', 'Newman', NULL, 'Sales', NULL);

Notice that if you provide NULL values instead of leaving the record blank, you can skip the column details on the first statement. You will no longer be required to specify the column names to be updated on the INSERT INTO statement.

Here is the updated table:

```
+--------+-----------+----------+------------+----------------+-----------+
| ID     | FIRSTNAME | LASTNAME | JOBTITLE   | DEPARTMENT     | MONTHLYPAY |
+--------+-----------+----------+------------+----------------+-----------+
| 190005 | John      | Watson   | Dispatcher | Administration |    5000.00 |
| 190006 | Mickey    | Malone   | Officer    | Operations     |    7000.00 |
| 190007 | Kirsten   | Dunk     | Manager    | Administration |    8000.00 |
| 190008 | Chinkee   | Stuart   | Agent      | Sales          |    6000.00 |
| 190009 | Sherry    | Lynx     | Executive  | NULL           |       NULL |
| 190010 | Julie     | Newman   | NULL       | Sales          |       NULL |
+--------+-----------+----------+------------+----------------+-----------+
6 rows in set (0.00 sec)
```

Summary

Tables serve as the primary storage tool in database systems. You can create a new table by using SQL's CREATE TABLE statement and specifying column definitions. You can also create a new table by copying the structures of an existing table using the CREATE TABLE statement with SELECT and FROM clauses.

77

You can populate a table with new data by using the INSERT INTO statement and specifying the data to be added using the VALUES clause. When adding a complete set of values for all columns, you may skip declaring the column names for the data. However, if you are adding values to specific columns, you will have to name the columns to be filled up. The values will be applied based on the order you have specified in the INSERT into statement.

Practice Exercises

Practice Exercise 6-1

Create a database and name it abccompany

Create a table and name it Sales2018

Provide the following specifications for the Sales2018 table:

Column Names	Description
ID	INTEGER, 6 DIGITS, AUTO_INCREMENT, NOT NULL
BRANCH	VARCHAR, 20 CHARACTERS, NOT NULL
PRODUCT_ID	INTEGER, 8 DIGITS
ANNUAL_SALES VALUE	INTEGER, 11 DIGITS, 2 DECIMALS,
REGION	VARCHAR, 15 CHARACTERS, NOT NULL
PRIMARY KEY	ID

Encode the following values to Sales2018 table:

Branch	Product_ID	Sales	Region
Arizona	1010	85,000.00	West
Arizona	1020	45,000.00	West
Utah	1010	55,000.00	West
Colorado	1010	34,500.00	West
Illinois	1010	44,500.00	Midwest

Ohio	1020	43,200.00	Midwest
Michigan	1010	25,000.00	Midwest
Michigan	1020	32,759.00	Midwest
Florida	1010	64,590.00	South
Georgia	1020	34,789.00	South
Maryland	1020	26,458.00	South
South Carolina	1010	29,874.00	South
Washington	1010	39,245.00	South
Washington	1020	63,589.00	South
Connecticut	1020	54,320.00	Northeast
New York	1010	42,569.00	Northeast
New York	1020	45,479.00	Northeast
Vermont	1010	54,368.00	Northeast
Massachusetts	1010	34,638.00	Northeast
Massachusetts	1020	34,876.00	Northeast

Use the SELECT command to display all data stored in SALES2018 table.

Practice Exercise 6-2

Create a new database and name it DATACLASS.

Define a new table with the name PRODUCTS. Use the following column definitions:

PRODUCTS TABLE	
Column Name	Data Type/Definition

PRODUCTID	Integer - 6 digits, NOT NULL
PRODNAME	VARCHAR, 30
PRICE	Decimal - 9 digits, 2 decimal places
INSTOCK	Integer - 7 digits
ONORDER	Integer - 7 digits
PRIMARY KEY	PRODUCTID

Show the structure of the PRODUCTS table.

Add the following data to the PRODUCTS table.

PRODUCTID	PRODNAME	PRICE	INSTOCK	ONORDER
101001	Butterfly Hinge 1	28.99	25	185
101002	Butterfly Hinge 2	32.44	30	0
101003	White Glue .5L	15.65	876	0
101004	White Glue 1L	28.99	874	0
101005	Drawer Runner .5	16.55	15	61
101006	Drawer Runner 1	30.27	410	0
101007	Deco Applique A	29.76	132	0
101008	Deco Applique B	25.77	212	92
101009	MDF Sheet	50.55	543	0
101010	Wood Frame	70.14	202	0

Show the entire data stored in PRODUCTS table.

Solutions

Practice Exercise 6-1

```
mysql> CREATE TABLE SALES2018(
    -> ID INT(6) AUTO_INCREMENT NOT NULL,
    -> BRANCH VARCHAR(20) NOT NULL,
    -> PRODUCT_ID INT(8) NOT NULL,
    -> ANNUAL_SALES DEC(11,2) NOT NULL,
    -> REGION VARCHAR(18) NOT NULL,
    -> PRIMARY KEY(ID)
    -> );
```

```
mysql> SELECT * FROM SALES2018;
+----+----------------+------------+--------------+-----------+
| ID | BRANCH         | PRODUCT_ID | ANNUAL_SALES | REGION    |
+----+----------------+------------+--------------+-----------+
|  1 | Arizona        |       1010 |     85000.00 | West      |
|  2 | Arizona        |       1020 |     45000.00 | West      |
|  3 | Utah           |       1010 |     55000.00 | West      |
|  4 | Colorado       |       1010 |     34500.00 | West      |
|  5 | Illinois       |       1010 |     44500.00 | Midwest   |
|  6 | Ohio           |       1020 |     43200.00 | Midwest   |
|  7 | Michigan       |       1010 |     25000.00 | Midwest   |
|  8 | Michigan       |       1020 |     32759.00 | Midwest   |
|  9 | Florida        |       1010 |     64590.00 | South     |
| 10 | Georgia        |       1020 |     34789.00 | South     |
| 11 | Maryland       |       1020 |     26458.00 | South     |
| 12 | South Carolina |       1010 |     29874.00 | South     |
| 13 | Washington     |       1010 |     39245.00 | South     |
| 14 | Washington     |       1020 |     63589.00 | South     |
| 15 | Connecticut    |       1020 |     54320.00 | Northeast |
| 16 | New York       |       1010 |     42569.00 | Northeast |
| 17 | New York       |       1020 |     45479.00 | Northeast |
| 18 | Vermont        |       1010 |     54368.00 | Northeast |
| 19 | Massachusetts  |       1010 |     34638.00 | Northeast |
| 20 | Massachusetts  |       1020 |     34876.00 | Northeast |
+----+----------------+------------+--------------+-----------+
20 rows in set (0.00 sec)
```

Practice Exercise 6-2

DESC PRODUCTS;

```
+-------------+---------------+------+-----+---------+-------+
| Field       | Type          | Null | Key | Default | Extra |
+-------------+---------------+------+-----+---------+-------+
| PRODUCTID   | int(6)        | NO   | PRI | NULL    |       |
| PRODNAME    | varchar(30)   | YES  |     | NULL    |       |
| PRICE       | decimal(9,2)  | YES  |     | NULL    |       |
| INSTOCK     | int(7)        | YES  |     | NULL    |       |
| ONORDER     | int(7)        | YES  |     | NULL    |       |
+-------------+---------------+------+-----+---------+-------+
5 rows in set (0.67 sec)
```

SELECT * FROM PRODUCTS;

```
+-----------+------------------+-------+---------+---------+
| PRODUCTID | PRODNAME         | PRICE | INSTOCK | ONORDER |
+-----------+------------------+-------+---------+---------+
|    101001 | Butterfly Hinge 1 | 28.99 |      25 |     185 |
|    101002 | Butterfly Hinge 2 | 32.44 |      30 |       0 |
|    101003 | White Glue .5L    | 15.65 |     876 |       0 |
|    101004 | White Glue 1L     | 28.99 |     874 |       0 |
|    101005 | Drawer Runner .5  | 16.55 |      15 |      61 |
|    101006 | Drawer Runner 1   | 30.27 |     410 |       0 |
|    101007 | Deco Applique A   | 29.76 |     132 |       0 |
|    101008 | Deco Applique B   | 25.77 |     212 |      92 |
|    101009 | MDF Sheet         | 50.55 |     543 |       0 |
|    101010 | Wood Frame        | 70.14 |     202 |       0 |
+-----------+------------------+-------+---------+---------+
10 rows in set (0.00 sec)
```

Chapter 7: Modifying and Removing Tables

At this point, you may have realized the value of carefully designing tables before putting them out for use. Erroneously designed tables can limit the usefulness of your database. Thankfully, SQL tables are not set in granite. In this chapter, you will learn how to change your table's name, columns, definitions, storage values, and other attributes.

The ALTER TABLE Command

The ALTER TABLE is a powerful command that will let you modify a table's name, structures, and definitions. You can use it to add new fields, remove columns, revise field definitions, change a table's storage value, and even include or exclude constraints.

This is the basic syntax for modifying a table:

```
ALTER TABLE TABLE_NAME [MODIFY] [COLUMN COLUMN_NAME][DATATYPE|NULL NOT NULL]
[RESTRICT|CASCADE]
                      [DROP]    [CONSTRAINT CONSTRAINT_NAME]
                      [ADD]     [COLUMN] COLUMN DEFINITION
```

Renaming a Table

To change a table's name, you will use the ALTER TABLE command with the RENAME function.

For example, if you want to change your table's name from EMPLOYEES to MEMBERS, the following statement will accomplish that purpose:

ALTER TABLE EMPLOYEES RENAME MEMBERS;

Modifying Column Attributes

A table's column attributes are the properties and behaviors set for all data entered in the column. This is typically defined at the time a table is created. If you find that the original design needs some improvement, you can still modify the column attributes much later using the ALTER TABLE command.

The ALTER TABLE command can be used to modify the following:

Column name

A column's data type

A column's size, scale, or precision

The use or omission of NULL values in columns

Renaming Columns

You may want to replace an existing column's name with a name that will reflect the nature of the data stored in that column.

Since you have already renamed the EMPLOYEES table to MEMBERS table, some columns may no longer be appropriate and you want those columns to be given the right name. The MEMBERS table has the following data:

```
+--------+-----------+----------+-----------+----------------+------------+
| ID     | FIRSTNAME | LASTNAME | JOBTITLE  | DEPARTMENT     | MONTHLYPAY |
+--------+-----------+----------+-----------+----------------+------------+
| 190005 | John      | Watson   | Dispatcher| Administration |    5000.00 |
| 190006 | Mickey    | Malone   | Officer   | Operations     |    7000.00 |
| 190007 | Kirsten   | Dunk     | Manager   | Administration |    8000.00 |
| 190008 | Chinkee   | Stuart   | Agent     | Sales          |    6000.00 |
| 190009 | Sherry    | Lynx     | Executive | Management     |   10000.00 |
+--------+-----------+----------+-----------+----------------+------------+
5 rows in set (0.74 sec)
```

The monthly pay column now seems unsuitable and you want to change it to ALLOWANCE to reflect the fact that each member listed on the table will be receiving an allowance and not a fixed salary. You may also want to change its data type from DECIMAL to an integer type with a maximum of 7 digits.

You will use this statement to rename the columns and change the data type at the same time:

ALTER TABLE MEMBERS CHANGE MONTHLYPAY ALLOWANCE INT(7);

Here is the result:

```
+--------+-----------+----------+-----------+----------------+-----------+
| ID     | FIRSTNAME | LASTNAME | JOBTITLE  | DEPARTMENT     | ALLOWANCE |
+--------+-----------+----------+-----------+----------------+-----------+
| 190005 | John      | Watson   | Dispatcher| Administration |      5000 |
| 190006 | Mickey    | Malone   | Officer   | Operations     |      7000 |
| 190007 | Kirsten   | Dunk     | Manager   | Administration |      8000 |
| 190008 | Chinkee   | Stuart   | Agent     | Sales          |      6000 |
| 190009 | Sherry    | Lynx     | Executive | Management     |     10000 |
+--------+-----------+----------+-----------+----------------+-----------+
```

Deleting a Column

Since the column JobTitle is no longer applicable, you can now drop this column using this statement:

ALTER TABLE MEMBERS
DROP COLUMN JobTitle;

Here is the updated MEMBERS table:

```
+---------+-----------+----------+----------------+-----------+
| ID      | FIRSTNAME | LASTNAME | DEPARTMENT     | ALLOWANCE |
+---------+-----------+----------+----------------+-----------+
| 190005  | John      | Watson   | Administration |      5000 |
| 190006  | Mickey    | Malone   | Operations     |      7000 |
| 190007  | Kirsten   | Dunk     | Administration |      8000 |
| 190008  | Chinkee   | Stuart   | Sales          |      6000 |
| 190009  | Sherry    | Lynx     | Management     |     10000 |
+---------+-----------+----------+----------------+-----------+
```

Adding a New Column

Since you will be working with a new set of data, you may want to add a new column on the MEMBERS table. For example, you can add a column that will store the membership type of each member. You can name the new column as MEMTYPE. This column will accept VARCHAR type with 15 characters.

You can use the following statement to add the MEMTYPE column:

ALTER TABLE MEMBERS ADD MEMTYPE VARCHAR(15);

Below is the updated MEMBERS table:

```
+--------+-----------+----------+----------------+-----------+---------+
| ID     | FIRSTNAME | LASTNAME | DEPARTMENT     | ALLOWANCE | MEMTYPE |
+--------+-----------+----------+----------------+-----------+---------+
| 190005 | John      | Watson   | Administration |      5000 | NULL    |
| 190006 | Mickey    | Malone   | Operations     |      7000 | NULL    |
| 190007 | Kirsten   | Dunk     | Administration |      8000 | NULL    |
| 190008 | Chinkee   | Stuart   | Sales          |      6000 | NULL    |
| 190009 | Sherry    | Lynx     | Management     |     10000 | NULL    |
+--------+-----------+----------+----------------+-----------+---------+
```

A new column, MEMTYPE, was added to the table and at this point, it has NULL values. Take note that you cannot add a new column with a NOT NULL value to a table with existing data or else, it will contradict its own constraint.

Modifying a Column's Definition

You can also combine the ALTER TABLE command with the MODIFY keyword to change the data type and specifications of a table without changing the column's name. To demonstrate, you can use the following statement to modify the data type of the column ALLOWANCE from an INT type to a DECIMAL type with up to 9 digits and two decimal places.

ALTER TABLE MEMBERS MODIFY ALLOWANCE DEC(9,2);

After all these changes, you may be curious to see the column names and attributes of the MEMBERS table. For this purpose, you can use the 'SHOW COLUMNS' statement to display the table's structure. Enter the following statement:

SHOW COLUMNS FROM MEMBERS;

Here is the result:

```
+--------------+--------------+------+-----+---------+-------+
| Field        | Type         | Null | Key | Default | Extra |
+--------------+--------------+------+-----+---------+-------+
| ID           | int(6)       | NO   |     | NULL    |       |
| FIRSTNAME    | varchar(20)  | NO   |     | NULL    |       |
| LASTNAME     | varchar(20)  | NO   |     | NULL    |       |
| DEPARTMENT   | varchar(15)  | YES  |     | NULL    |       |
| ALLOWANCE    | decimal(9,2) | YES  |     | NULL    |       |
| MEMTYPE      | varchar(15)  | YES  |     | NULL    |       |
+--------------+--------------+------+-----+---------+-------+
```

Important Reminders about the ALTER TABLE Command

Adding Columns to a Database Table

When adding a new column, remember that you cannot append a column with a NOT NULL attribute to a table with existing data. In general, you will need to specify a column to be NOT NULL to indicate that it will hold a value. Adding a NOT NULL column will contradict the constraint as the new column does not come with data.

Modifying Fields/Columns

The following rules apply when modifying existing columns:

91

- You may only decrease a column's size if the current size is equal to or shorter than the desired size for the column. However, you can always increase its size.

- You can modify the data type of a column anytime.

- You can adjust the decimal places of numeric data type as long as the desired figure does not exceed the maximum allowable decimal places.

- You can easily increase the precision of numeric data types but you will only be able to decrease it if the largest precision is equal to or higher than the desired precision.

The ALTER TABLE command is a valuable command that you can use to modify your tables in different ways. However, the inadvertent use of this command can have disastrous results on your database. You have to make sure that you are dropping the right column or you could lose valuable data.

Deleting Tables

The DROP TABLE command is used to remove a table and its definitions from a database. Dropping a table will also remove its data, associated index, triggers, constraints, and permission data.

Syntax:

DROP TABLE table_name;

For example, to delete the MEMBERS table from the database, you will use this statement:

DROP TABLE MEMBERS;

Executing the DROP TABLE command will remove the MEMBERS table and its attributes and definitions.

Summary

The ALTER TABLE statement is SQL's maintenance command. It can be used to modify and refine your table in many different ways. You will use it to rename a table, modify column definition, rename a column, add a new column, and remove an existing column. The DROP TABLE command is used to remove a table and its attributes from the database.

Practice Exercises

Practice Exercises 7-1

Change the active database to DATACLASS. This is the database you created in Practice Exercise 6-2.

Create a new table with the following definitions and name it PURCHASE table:

PURCHASE TABLE	
Column Name	Data Type
ORDERNO	Integer - 8 digits, NOT NULL
ORDERDATE	Date
PRODUCTID	Integer - 6 digits
VOLUME	Integer – 5
PRICE	Decimal - 9 digits, 2 decimal places

TOTAL	Decimal - 9 digits, 2 decimal places
PRIMARY KEY	ORDERNO

Populate the PURCHASE table with the following data:

ORDERNO	ORDERDATE	PRODUCTID	VOLUME	PRICE	TOTAL
20100123	09/01/2019	101001	98	28.99	2841.02
20100124	09/05/2019	101005	46	16.55	761.3
20100125	09/07/2019	101001	87	14.98	1303.26
20100126	09/10/2019	101008	92	25.77	2370.84
20100127	09/11/2019	101005	15	78.32	1174.8

Display the entire content of the PURCHASE Table

Change the name of the table from PURCHASE to ORDERS.

Change the Column Name Volume to Quantity and adjust its size to 6 digits.

Remove the TOTAL column from the ORDERS table.

Display the updated content of the ORDERS table.

Solution

Practice Exercises 7-1

USE DATACLASS;

CREATE TABLE PURCHASE(
ORDERNO INT(8) NOT NULL,
ORDERDATE DATE,
PRODUCTID INT(6),
VOLUME INT(5),
PRICE DECIMAL (9,2),
TOTAL DECIMAL(9,2),
PRIMARY KEY(ORDERNO)
);

Populate the new table with given data:

```
mysql> INSERT INTO PURCHASE
    -> VALUES(20100124, 20190905, 101005, 46, 16.55, 761.30);
Query OK, 1 row affected (0.17 sec)

mysql> INSERT INTO PURCHASE
    -> VALUES(20100125, 20190907, 101001, 87, 14.98, 1303.26);
Query OK, 1 row affected (0.11 sec)

mysql> INSERT INTO PURCHASE
    -> VALUES(20100126, 20190910, 101008, 92, 25.77, 2370.84);
Query OK, 1 row affected (0.17 sec)

mysql> INSERT INTO PURCHASE
    -> VALUES(20100127, 20190911, 101005, 15, 78.32, 1174.8);
Query OK, 1 row affected (0.12 sec)
```

SELECT * FROM PURCHASE;

```
+----------+------------+-----------+--------+-------+---------+
| ORDERNO  | ORDERDATE  | PRODUCTID | VOLUME | PRICE | TOTAL   |
+----------+------------+-----------+--------+-------+---------+
| 20100123 | 2019-09-01 |    101001 |     98 | 28.99 | 2841.02 |
| 20100124 | 2019-09-05 |    101005 |     46 | 16.55 |  761.30 |
| 20100125 | 2019-09-07 |    101001 |     87 | 14.98 | 1303.26 |
| 20100126 | 2019-09-10 |    101008 |     92 | 25.77 | 2370.84 |
| 20100127 | 2019-09-11 |    101005 |     15 | 78.32 | 1174.80 |
+----------+------------+-----------+--------+-------+---------+
5 rows in set (0.07 sec)
```

Rename the PURCHASE table as ORDERS table:

ALTER TABLE PURCHASE RENAME ORDERS;

Change Column the column name VOLUME to QUANTITY and adjust its Integer size to 6:

ALTER TABLE ORDERS CHANGE VOLUME QUANTITY INT(6);

Remove the TOTAL column:

ALTER TABLE ORDERS
DROP COLUMN TOTAL;

Show the updated ORDERS table:

SELECT * FROM ORDERS;

```
+----------+------------+-----------+----------+-------+
| ORDERNO  | ORDERDATE  | PRODUCTID | QUANTITY | PRICE |
+----------+------------+-----------+----------+-------+
| 20100123 | 2019-09-01 |    101001 |       98 | 28.99 |
| 20100124 | 2019-09-05 |    101005 |       46 | 16.55 |
| 20100125 | 2019-09-07 |    101001 |       87 | 14.98 |
| 20100126 | 2019-09-10 |    101008 |       92 | 25.77 |
| 20100127 | 2019-09-11 |    101005 |       15 | 78.32 |
+----------+------------+-----------+----------+-------+
5 rows in set (0.01 sec)
```

Chapter 8: Performing Queries

The Data Query Language consists of only one command: SELECT. The SELECT command is used to execute queries in relational databases. It can be combined with other clauses to retrieve results that are more detailed.

In the preceding chapter, you learned how to use the SELECT command to return a set of data. In this chapter, you will learn a lot more about this powerful command. You will know how to use SELECT in database queries to retrieve any data you may need.

Performing Queries

What are Queries?

Queries are inquiries made into a database. In SQL, queries are made through the SELECT command. The SELECT command is used to search for and display data stored in a database. For example, if your database has a table with sales information, you can launch a query to find out the bestselling product, the top selling salesman, the top buyer, etc. Modern relational databases are set up to provide highly useful data on demand through queries.

The SELECT Command

The SELECT command is the primary command for performing queries on a database. It is commonly paired with other SQL clauses to launch precise and more detailed queries. Some clauses are mandatory. The optional clauses are provided to improve the effectiveness of queries.

The SELECT cause is used to specify the records that you want to fetch from a database. It is used to indicate the columns(s) that will serve as the basis for the search.

The FROM keyword

The FROM keyword is a mandatory element of a database query. It is used to name the source table for the data that you want to retrieve. It requires at least one table as argument.

A basic query uses this syntax:

```
SELECT column1, column2, column3 FROM table_name;
```

To demonstrate, you will be using the EMPLOYEES table with the following data:

```
+--------+-----------+----------+------------+----------------+-----------+
| ID     | FIRSTNAME | LASTNAME | JOBTITLE   | DEPARTMENT     | MONTHLYPAY |
+--------+-----------+----------+------------+----------------+-----------+
| 190005 | John      | Watson   | Dispatcher | Administration |   5000.00 |
| 190006 | Mickey    | Malone   | Officer    | Operations     |   7000.00 |
| 190007 | Kirsten   | Dunk     | Manager    | Administration |   8000.00 |
| 190008 | Chinkee   | Stuart   | Agent      | Sales          |   6000.00 |
| 190009 | Sherry    | Lynx     | Executive  | Management     |  10000.00 |
+--------+-----------+----------+------------+----------------+-----------+
5 rows in set (1.17 sec)
```

If you want to retrieve the data for the columns FIRSTNAME, LASTNAME, and MONTHLY PAY, here is how you can write the query statement:

SELECT FIRSTNAME, LASTNAME, MONTHLYPAY FROM EMPLOYEES;

Here is the result:

```
+----------+----------+------------+
| FIRSTNAME | LASTNAME | MONTHLYPAY |
+----------+----------+------------+
| John     | Watson   |    5000.00 |
| Mickey   | Malone   |    7000.00 |
| Kirsten  | Dunk     |    8000.00 |
| Chinkee  | Stuart   |    6000.00 |
| Sherry   | Lynx     |   10000.00 |
+----------+----------+------------+
5 rows in set (0.09 sec)
```

Notice that the columns were displayed based on the order they were listed in the SELECT statement.

Modifying Queries

SQL offers some modifiers that you can apply to make queries more useful. You can limit the records to be displayed, set filters, and arrange data.

Limiting Output Using the LIMIT Clause

If you are operating a large database, you may be using tables with thousands of records. Hence, a standard query on the table's content may also yield thousands of rows. Such query can consume your resources and cause the query to lag. For a smoother query operation, you may choose to limit the number of results to be displayed by the query. You can use the LIMIT clause for that purpose.

For example, if you want to view only the first three rows in the EMPLOYEES table, you can execute this statement:

SELECT * FROM EMPLOYEES
LIMIT 3;

Here is the result:

```
+--------+-----------+----------+------------+----------------+------------+
| ID     | FIRSTNAME | LASTNAME | JOBTITLE   | DEPARTMENT     | MONTHLYPAY |
+--------+-----------+----------+------------+----------------+------------+
| 190005 | John      | Watson   | Dispatcher | Administration |    5000.00 |
| 190006 | Mickey    | Malone   | Officer    | Operations     |    7000.00 |
| 190007 | Kirsten   | Dunk     | Manager    | Administration |    8000.00 |
+--------+-----------+----------+------------+----------------+------------+
3 rows in set (0.00 sec)
```

Filtering Data Using the WHERE Clause

The WHERE clause is used to refine queries by allowing users to specify one or more conditions. The selected values are returned only if the specified condition is satisfied.

You can use the WHERE clause to perform operations such as launching queries, updating records, and joining multiple tables. You will use this keyword to filter data and display your selected records. It is commonly paired with commands like SELECT, UPDATE, and DELETE.

The WHERE clause takes single or multiple conditions to refine the query. If you want to use multiple conditions you will need to connect them with SQL operators such as OR, AND, =, <, >, or LIKE.

Here is the syntax for the SELECT command with a WHERE keyword:

```
SELECT column1, column2, column3
FROM table_name
WHERE [condition];
```

To see how it works, you can filter the EMPLOYEES table to display the first name and last name of employees whose salary is higher than 7,000. Here is the statement:

SELECT LASTNAME, FIRSTNAME, MONTHLYPAY FROM EMPLOYEES
WHERE MONTHLYPAY >7000.00;

Output:

```
+-------------+-------------+-------------+
| LASTNAME    | FIRSTNAME   | MONTHLYPAY  |
+-------------+-------------+-------------+
| Dunk        | Kirsten     |     8000.00 |
| Lynx        | Sherry      |    10000.00 |
+-------------+-------------+-------------+
2 rows in set (0.10 sec)
```

Since only two employees matched the requirement, the query generated two rows of data showing the Last Name, First Name, and Monthly Pay.

Arranging Data Using ORDER BY

Normally, you want to see data from a table in a certain order. In SQL, you can sort the output of a query in either descending order or descending order using the ORDER BY clause. If you do not specify a sorting order, it will return the data in an ascending order. For example, if you are working with text or character types, the result will be displayed alphabetically by default.

Syntax:

```
SELECT column1, column2
FROM table_name
[WHERE condition]
[ORDER BY column1, column2] [ASC | DESC];
```

To see how it works, you can sort the EMPLOYEES table in ascending order based on the last name columns with the following statement:

SELECT * FROM EMPLOYEES
ORDER BY LASTNAME ASC;

Here is the output:

```
+--------+-----------+----------+------------+----------------+------------+
| ID     | FIRSTNAME | LASTNAME | JOBTITLE   | DEPARTMENT     | MONTHLYPAY |
+--------+-----------+----------+------------+----------------+------------+
| 190007 | Kirsten   | Dunk     | Manager    | Administration |    8000.00 |
| 190009 | Sherry    | Lynx     | Executive  | Management     |   10000.00 |
| 190006 | Mickey    | Malone   | Officer    | Operations     |    7000.00 |
| 190008 | Chinkee   | Stuart   | Agent      | Sales          |    6000.00 |
| 190005 | John      | Watson   | Dispatcher | Administration |    5000.00 |
+--------+-----------+----------+------------+----------------+------------+
5 rows in set (0.09 sec)
```

This time, you can try to sort the data in the EMPLOYEES table in descending order based on the employees' monthly pay. You can use the following statement for this purpose:

SELECT * FROM EMPLOYEES
ORDER BY MONTHLYPAY DESC;

Output:

```
+--------+-----------+----------+-----------+----------------+-----------+
| ID     | FIRSTNAME | LASTNAME | JOBTITLE  | DEPARTMENT     | MONTHLYPAY |
+--------+-----------+----------+-----------+----------------+-----------+
| 190005 | John      | Watson   | Dispatcher| Administration |    5000.00 |
| 190008 | Chinkee   | Stuart   | Agent     | Sales          |    6000.00 |
| 190006 | Mickey    | Malone   | Officer   | Operations     |    7000.00 |
| 190009 | Sherry    | Lynx     | Executive | Management     |   10000.00 |
| 190007 | Kirsten   | Dunk     | Manager   | Administration |    8000.00 |
+--------+-----------+----------+-----------+----------------+-----------+
5 rows in set (0.00 sec)
```

Grouping Data with the GROUP BY Clause

The GROUP BY clause is another keyword that you can use with the SELECT command to perform more useful queries from a table. The GROUP BY clause lets you arrange the query results based off a single or multiple columns. This is frequently combined with functions such as COUNT, SUM, AVG, MAX, and MIN. You will learn more about these functions in another chapter.

If you are going to use the GROUP BY clause with the ORDER BY and WHERE clause, do make sure that the GROUP BY clause is placed before the ORDER BY clause and after the WHERE clause.

Syntax for GROUP BY clause with ORDER BY and WHERE

```
SELECT column1, column2, ....
FROM table_name
WHERE condition
GROUP BY column1, column2..
ORDER BY column1, column2...;
```

To demonstrate how the GROUP BY clause works with the SELECT command and other clauses, you will use the Sales2018 table with the following information:

```
+----+----------------+------------+--------------+-----------+
| ID | BRANCH         | PRODUCT_ID | ANNUAL_SALES | REGION    |
+----+----------------+------------+--------------+-----------+
|  1 | Arizona        |       1010 |     85000.00 | West      |
|  2 | Arizona        |       1020 |     45000.00 | West      |
|  3 | Utah           |       1010 |     55000.00 | West      |
|  4 | Colorado       |       1010 |     34500.00 | West      |
|  5 | Illinois       |       1010 |     44500.00 | Midwest   |
|  6 | Ohio           |       1020 |     43200.00 | Midwest   |
|  7 | Michigan       |       1010 |     25000.00 | Midwest   |
|  8 | Michigan       |       1020 |     32759.00 | Midwest   |
|  9 | Florida        |       1010 |     64590.00 | South     |
| 10 | Georgia        |       1020 |     34789.00 | South     |
| 11 | Maryland       |       1020 |     26458.00 | South     |
| 12 | South Carolina |       1010 |     29874.00 | South     |
| 13 | Washington     |       1010 |     39245.00 | South     |
| 14 | Washington     |       1020 |     63589.00 | South     |
| 15 | Connecticut    |       1020 |     54320.00 | Northeast |
| 16 | New York       |       1010 |     42569.00 | Northeast |
| 17 | New York       |       1020 |     45479.00 | Northeast |
| 18 | Vermont        |       1010 |     54368.00 | Northeast |
| 19 | Massachusetts  |       1010 |     34638.00 | Northeast |
| 20 | Massachusetts  |       1020 |     34876.00 | Northeast |
+----+----------------+------------+--------------+-----------+
20 rows in set (0.19 sec)
```

You can use the GROUP BY clause to extract value information from the Sales2018.

For example, if you want to obtain the sales per region, you can run this statement:

SELECT Region, SUM(ANNUAL_SALES)
FROM SALES2018
GROUP BY REGION;

Take note that the above query uses the SUM operator to get the total sales. The GROUP BY clause was used to display the result by region.

Output:

```
+------------+---------------------+
| REGION     | SUM(ANNUAL_SALES)   |
+------------+---------------------+
| West       |          219500.00  |
| Midwest    |          145459.00  |
| South      |          258545.00  |
| Northeast  |          266250.00  |
+------------+---------------------+
4 rows in set (0.15 sec)
```

The query returned four rows showing the four regions with their corresponding sales.

Let's say you want to find out the total sales per product, you can execute this statement:

SELECT PRODUCT_ID, SUM(ANNUAL_SALES)
FROM SALES2018
GROUP BY PRODUCT_ID;

Output:

```
+------------+-------------------+
| PRODUCT_ID | SUM(ANNUAL_SALES) |
+------------+-------------------+
|       1010 |         509284.00 |
|       1020 |         380470.00 |
+------------+-------------------+
2 rows in set (0.00 sec)
```

This time, the query returned two rows showing the total sales per product.

If you want to know the sales performance of each product for each region, you can specify multiple columns with the GROUP BY clause.

For example, the following statement will group the specified information by REGION and PRODUCT_ID:

SELECT REGION, PRODUCT_ID, SUM(ANNUAL_SALES)
FROM SALES2018
GROUP BY REGION, PRODUCT_ID;

Output:

```
+-------------+------------+--------------------+
| REGION      | PRODUCT_ID | SUM(ANNUAL_SALES)  |
+-------------+------------+--------------------+
| West        |       1010 |          174500.00 |
| West        |       1020 |           45000.00 |
| Midwest     |       1010 |           69500.00 |
| Midwest     |       1020 |           75959.00 |
| South       |       1010 |          133709.00 |
| South       |       1020 |          124836.00 |
| Northeast   |       1020 |          134675.00 |
| Northeast   |       1010 |          131575.00 |
+-------------+------------+--------------------+
8 rows in set (0.00 sec)
```

The query returned 8 rows of data and displayed the sales per product and per region.

You may want to see how each branch is doing in terms of total sales. You can easily do that with the GROUP BY clause:

SELECT BRANCH, SUM(ANNUAL_SALES)
FROM SALES2018
GROUP BY BRANCH;

Output:

```
+------------------------+------------------------+
| BRANCH                 | SUM(ANNUAL_SALES)      |
+------------------------+------------------------+
| Arizona                |            130000.00   |
| Utah                   |             55000.00   |
| Colorado               |             34500.00   |
| Illinois               |             44500.00   |
| Ohio                   |             43200.00   |
| Michigan               |             57759.00   |
| Florida                |             64590.00   |
| Georgia                |             34789.00   |
| Maryland               |             26458.00   |
| South Carolina         |             29874.00   |
| Washington             |            102834.00   |
| Connecticut            |             54320.00   |
| New York               |             88048.00   |
| Vermont                |             54368.00   |
| Massachusetts          |             69514.00   |
+------------------------+------------------------+
15 rows in set (0.03 sec)
```

So far, you have been using the GROUP BY clause with the SUM function. You can also use the GROUP BY clause with multiple functions. For example, on top of the total annual sales for each

113

product per region, you may also want to view the average sales for each product per region.

You can use this statement to extract the desired information:

SELECT REGION, PRODUCT_ID, SUM(ANNUAL_SALES), AVG(ANNUAL_SALES)
FROM SALES2018
GROUP BY REGION, PRODUCT_ID;

Output:

```
+-----------+------------+-------------------+-------------------+
| REGION    | PRODUCT_ID | SUM(ANNUAL_SALES) | AVG(ANNUAL_SALES) |
+-----------+------------+-------------------+-------------------+
| West      |       1010 |         174500.00 |      58166.666667 |
| West      |       1020 |          45000.00 |      45000.000000 |
| Midwest   |       1010 |          69500.00 |      34750.000000 |
| Midwest   |       1020 |          75959.00 |      37979.500000 |
| South     |       1010 |         133709.00 |      44569.666667 |
| South     |       1020 |         124836.00 |      41612.000000 |
| Northeast |       1020 |         134675.00 |      44891.666667 |
| Northeast |       1010 |         131575.00 |      43858.333333 |
+-----------+------------+-------------------+-------------------+
8 rows in set (0.04 sec)
```

Summary:

The SELECT statement is the main query tool for SQL. It is used to search and display data stored in a table. The SELECT command is used with the FROM keyword to identify the query's target table.

You can use several clauses to modify the results of the query. The LIMIT clause is used to specify the number of rows to be displayed in the query. The WHERE clause is used to refine the query result based on the specified condition. The ORDER BY clause is used to arrange the results of the query on ascending or descending order. The GROUP BY clause lets you arrange data based on field values.

SQL supports functions and operators like AVG() and SUM() and you can use them to return meaningful and useful results from your queries.

Practice Exercises

Practice Exercise 8-1

For this Exercise, you will be using the ORDERS table from the DATACLASS database with the following data:

```
+----------+------------+-----------+----------+--------+
| ORDERNO  | ORDERDATE  | PRODUCTID | QUANTITY | PRICE  |
+----------+------------+-----------+----------+--------+
| 20100123 | 2019-09-01 |    101001 |       98 | 28.99  |
| 20100124 | 2019-09-05 |    101005 |       46 | 16.55  |
| 20100125 | 2019-09-07 |    101001 |       87 | 14.98  |
| 20100126 | 2019-09-10 |    101008 |       92 | 25.77  |
| 20100127 | 2019-09-11 |    101005 |       15 | 78.32  |
+----------+------------+-----------+----------+--------+
```

Write a query that will return the ORDER Number, Product ID, and Quantity for the first four orders in the table.

Write a query that will return all column values for orders with quantity that exceed 50.

Write a query that will sort the rows on ascending order based on the PRODUCT ID.

Write a query that will sort the rows on descending order based on the PRICE values.

Write a query that will return the Product ID and the total order quantity per product.

Solution:

Practice Exercise 8-1

SELECT ORDERNO, PRODUCTID, QUANTITY FROM
ORDERS
LIMIT 4;

```
+-----------+-------------+------------+
| ORDERNO   | PRODUCTID   | QUANTITY   |
+-----------+-------------+------------+
| 20100123  |      101001 |         98 |
| 20100124  |      101005 |         46 |
| 20100125  |      101001 |         87 |
| 20100126  |      101008 |         92 |
+-----------+-------------+------------+
4 rows in set (0.00 sec)
```

SELECT * FROM ORDERS
WHERE QUANTITY > 50

```
+-----------+-------------+-------------+------------+---------+
| ORDERNO   | ORDERDATE   | PRODUCTID   | QUANTITY   | PRICE   |
+-----------+-------------+-------------+------------+---------+
| 20100123  | 2019-09-01  |      101001 |         98 |   28.99 |
| 20100125  | 2019-09-07  |      101001 |         87 |   14.98 |
| 20100126  | 2019-09-10  |      101008 |         92 |   25.77 |
+-----------+-------------+-------------+------------+---------+
3 rows in set (0.00 sec)
```

SELECT * FROM ORDERS
ORDER BY PRODUCTID ASC;

117

```
+----------+------------+-----------+----------+-------+
| ORDERNO  | ORDERDATE  | PRODUCTID | QUANTITY | PRICE |
+----------+------------+-----------+----------+-------+
| 20100123 | 2019-09-01 |    101001 |       98 | 28.99 |
| 20100125 | 2019-09-07 |    101001 |       87 | 14.98 |
| 20100124 | 2019-09-05 |    101005 |       46 | 16.55 |
| 20100127 | 2019-09-11 |    101005 |       15 | 78.32 |
| 20100126 | 2019-09-10 |    101008 |       92 | 25.77 |
+----------+------------+-----------+----------+-------+
5 rows in set (0.00 sec)
```

SELECT * FROM ORDERS

ORDER BY PRICE DESC;

```
+----------+------------+-----------+----------+-------+
| ORDERNO  | ORDERDATE  | PRODUCTID | QUANTITY | PRICE |
+----------+------------+-----------+----------+-------+
| 20100127 | 2019-09-11 |    101005 |       15 | 78.32 |
| 20100123 | 2019-09-01 |    101001 |       98 | 28.99 |
| 20100126 | 2019-09-10 |    101008 |       92 | 25.77 |
| 20100124 | 2019-09-05 |    101005 |       46 | 16.55 |
| 20100125 | 2019-09-07 |    101001 |       87 | 14.98 |
+----------+------------+-----------+----------+-------+
5 rows in set (0.00 sec)
```

SELECT PRODUCTID, SUM(QUANTITY)

FROM ORDERS

GROUP BY PRODUCTID;

```
+-----------+----------------+
| PRODUCTID | SUM(QUANTITY)  |
+-----------+----------------+
|    101001 |            185 |
|    101005 |             61 |
|    101008 |             92 |
+-----------+----------------+
3 rows in set (0.24 sec)
```

Chapter 9: Updating, Removing, and Inserting Data

Tables store data and records that change over time or become obsolete. SQL provides important commands that you can use to modify, replace, or delete your records as well as append new ones.

The Data Manipulation Language (DML) category of SQL offers three commands that you can use to remove, update, and insert rows in tables.

Command	Usage
UPDATE	Updates or modifies existing data
DELETE	Deletes rows or records in a table
INSERT	Inserts or adds a row of data into a table

Updating Data

The UPDATE Command

The UPDATE command is used to modify records in tables. You can use it to change one or more rows. This command is used to modify an existing record.

The UPDATE command is used with the SET keyword to specify the columns to be modified and the corresponding value. It is usually qualified by the WHERE clause, a modifier which specifies the criteria for the record to be updated.

Syntax:

```
UPDATE table_name
SET column1=value1, column2=value2
WHERE some_column=value;
```

In the above statement, the UPDATE command specifies the name of the table to be updated. The SET clause indicates the columns to be updated and their corresponding values. The WHERE clause defines the condition(s) and sets the restrictions for the record(s) to be updated.

Be warned that omitting the WHERE clause will cause all records to be updated.

To demonstrate, you will be using the EMPLOYEES table with the following data:

```
+--------+-----------+----------+-----------+----------------+-----------+
| ID     | FIRSTNAME | LASTNAME | JOBTITLE  | DEPARTMENT     | MONTHLYPAY |
+--------+-----------+----------+-----------+----------------+-----------+
| 190005 | John      | Watson   | Dispatcher| Administration |   5000.00 |
| 190006 | Mickey    | Malone   | Officer   | Operations     |   7000.00 |
| 190007 | Kirsten   | Dunk     | Manager   | Administration |   8000.00 |
| 190008 | Chinkee   | Stuart   | Agent     | Sales          |   6000.00 |
| 190009 | Sherry    | Lynx     | Executive | Management     |  10000.00 |
+--------+-----------+----------+-----------+----------------+-----------+
5 rows in set (1.17 sec)
```

For example, assuming you want to update the data for the DEPARTMENT and MONTHLY PAY for the employee named Sherry Lynx to their current values, you can execute this statement:

UPDATE EMPLOYEES
SET DEPARTMENT='Sales', MONTHLYPAY=8000.00
WHERE LASTNAME='Lynx';

Output:

```
+--------+-----------+----------+-----------+----------------+------------+
| ID     | FIRSTNAME | LASTNAME | JOBTITLE  | DEPARTMENT     | MONTHLYPAY |
+--------+-----------+----------+-----------+----------------+------------+
| 190005 | John      | Watson   | Dispatcher| Administration |    5000.00 |
| 190006 | Mickey    | Malone   | Officer   | Operations     |    7000.00 |
| 190007 | Kirsten   | Dunk     | Manager   | Administration |    8000.00 |
| 190008 | Chinkee   | Stuart   | Agent     | Sales          |    6000.00 |
| 190009 | Sherry    | Lynx     | Executive | Sales          |    8000.00 |
+--------+-----------+----------+-----------+----------------+------------+
5 rows in set (0.00 sec)
```

The DEPARTMENT and MONTHLYPAY column values for the employee named Sherry Lynx now reflect the values specified in the SET clause.

Removing Rows

At some point, you may need to discard a record or a row of data from a table. You can do this through the DELETE command.

The DELETE Command

The DELETE command is used to eliminate an entire row of information. The DELETE statement is commonly used with the WHERE clause to specify the criteria for deletion. There is always a risk of accidentally deleting the wrong record so you have to be cautious when executing the DELETE command.

123

Syntax:

```
DELETE FROM table_name
WHERE column=somevalue;
```

The WHERE clause is used with the DELETE command to set which record is up for deletion. Take note that omitting the WHERE clause can cause the deletion of all records in the specified table.

Ideally, disasters like accidental deletion can be overturned or mitigated by restoring a recent backup of your files. If you have been performing regular backups on a secure location, it may mean less recovery work. In worse scenario, you may have to manually input data, which could be time consuming if you are working with tons of records.

To demonstrate the use of the DELETE command, you can use the EMPLOYEES table:

```
+--------+-----------+----------+------------+----------------+-----------+
| ID     | FIRSTNAME | LASTNAME | JOBTITLE   | DEPARTMENT     | MONTHLYPAY |
+--------+-----------+----------+------------+----------------+-----------+
| 190005 | John      | Watson   | Dispatcher | Administration |   5000.00 |
| 190006 | Mickey    | Malone   | Officer    | Operations     |   7000.00 |
| 190007 | Kirsten   | Dunk     | Manager    | Administration |   8000.00 |
| 190008 | Chinkee   | Stuart   | Agent      | Sales          |   6000.00 |
| 190009 | Sherry    | Lynx     | Executive  | Sales          |   8000.00 |
+--------+-----------+----------+------------+----------------+-----------+
5 rows in set (0.00 sec)
```

To delete the records of the employee named "Sherry Lynx, you will use this DELETE statement with the WHERE clause:

DELETE FROM EMPLOYEES
WHERE LAST_NAME = 'Lynx'

Output:

```
+--------+-----------+----------+------------+----------------+-----------+
| ID     | FIRSTNAME | LASTNAME | JOBTITLE   | DEPARTMENT     | MONTHLYPAY |
+--------+-----------+----------+------------+----------------+-----------+
| 190005 | John      | Watson   | Dispatcher | Administration |   5000.00 |
| 190006 | Mickey    | Malone   | Officer    | Operations     |   7000.00 |
| 190007 | Kirsten   | Dunk     | Manager    | Administration |   8000.00 |
| 190008 | Chinkee   | Stuart   | Agent      | Sales          |   6000.00 |
+--------+-----------+----------+------------+----------------+-----------+
4 rows in set (0.00 sec)
```

The updated EMPLOYEES table now only shows four remaining records.

Deleting all Data

The DELETE command is also used to remove all records in a table without removing the table itself. You can do this by omitting the WHERE clause in the DELETE statement.

Syntax:

DELETE FROM table_name;

The above statement will remove all existing data from the table but the table will retain its structures and attributes and you can still add new records later if you want to.

You can delete the entire content of the EMPLOYEES table with this statement:

DELETE FROM EMPLOYEES;

To see the effect of the DELETE statement on the EMPLOYEES table, you can run a query with this statement:

SELECT * FROM EMPLOYEES;

Output:

```
mysql> SELECT * FROM EMPLOYEES;
Empty set (0.00 sec)
```

The query returned an empty set.

Inserting Data

The INSERT Command

The INSERT command is used to add a new record to a table. You can either add data to all columns or add data to specific columns.

If you want to add a set of data corresponding to all columns, you will use the following syntax:

```
INSERT INTO table_name
VALUES ('value1', 'value2'... [NULL];
```

The above data is only applicable if you have a complete set of data for each of the columns in the table.

On the other hand, if you have to add data to selected columns, you will have to specify the columns names as indicated by this syntax:

```
INSERT INTO table_name (column1, column2, column3)
VALUES ('value1', 'value2', 'value3');
```

The values provided are assigned based on the specified order of the columns.

```
INSERT INTO table_name (column1, column2, column3)
VALUES ('value1', 'value2', 'value3');
```

To demonstrate, you can create a new table called CUSTOMERS.

The CUSTOMERS table has the following definitions:

CUSTOMERID	INTEGER, 6, NOT NULL
CUSTNAME	VARCHAR, 35, NOT NULL
TITLE	VARCHAR, 20
ADDRESS	VARCHAR, 50
CITY	VARCHAR, 25
STATE	VARCHAR, 25
PRIMARY KEY	CUSTOMERID

Add the following data to the CUSTOMERS table:

CUSTOMERID	CUSTNAME	TITLE	ADDRESS	CITY	STATE
9999102	John Wells	Mr.	5055 Harbour Lake Dr	Goose Creek	SC
9999104	Steven Martin	Mr.	114 Smith Ln	Raceland	LA
9999106	Elsa Morana	Ms.	1590 Shaffer Rd	Atwater	CA
9999125	Daisy King	Ms.	1181 E Walnut St	Carbondale	IL
9999126	Daniel Bean	Mr.	205 N 10th Ave	Hill City	KS

Display all data for the CUSTOMERS table:

SELECT * FROM CUSTOMERS;

Output:

```
+-----------+---------------+-------+----------------------+-------------+-------+
| CUSTOMERID | CUSTNAME     | TITLE | ADDRESS              | CITY        | STATE |
+-----------+---------------+-------+----------------------+-------------+-------+
|   9999102 | John Wells    | Mr.   | 5055 Harbour Lake Dr.| Goose Creek | SC    |
|   9999104 | Steven Martin | Mr.   | 114 Smith Ln         | Raceland    | LA    |
|   9999106 | Elsa Morana   | Ms.   | 1590 Shaffer Rd      | Atwater     | CA    |
|   9999125 | Daisy King    | Ms.   | 1181 E Walnut St.    | Carbondale  | IL    |
|   9999126 | Daniel Bean   | Mr.   | 205 N 10th Ave       | Hill City   | KS    |
+-----------+---------------+-------+----------------------+-------------+-------+
5 rows in set (0.00 sec)
```

Summary:

SQL's Data Manipulation Language (DML) provides three main commands that you can use to remove, update, and add data to tables. The UPDATE statement is used to modify existing records. The DELETE statement is used to remove rows of data from a table. The INSERT statement is used to add new rows of data to a table.

Practice Exercises

Practice Exercise 9-1

For this exercise, you will use the table ORDERS from the CLASSDATA database, which contains the following data:

```
+----------+------------+-----------+----------+--------+
| ORDERNO  | ORDERDATE  | PRODUCTID | QUANTITY | PRICE  |
+----------+------------+-----------+----------+--------+
| 20100123 | 2019-09-01 |   101001  |       98 | 28.99  |
| 20100124 | 2019-09-05 |   101005  |       46 | 16.55  |
| 20100125 | 2019-09-07 |   101001  |       87 | 14.98  |
| 20100126 | 2019-09-10 |   101008  |       92 | 25.77  |
| 20100127 | 2019-09-11 |   101005  |       15 | 78.32  |
+----------+------------+-----------+----------+--------+
```

The following Order Numbers have PRICE values that need correction:

ORDER No.	Correct Price
20100125	28.99
20100127	16.55

Write the statements that will modify the value for the above Orders.

Show the updated ORDERS table.

Practice Exercise 9-2

Add the following data to the ORDERS table:

ORDERNO	ORDERDATE	PRODUCTID	VOLUME	PRICE
20100128	09/12/2019	101008	98	25.77
20100129	09/13/2019	101009	46	50.55
20100130	09/14/2019	101001	87	28.99
20100131	09/20/2019	101007	92	29.76
20100132	09/21/2019	101009	15	50.55

Show the updated ORDERS table.

Practice Exercise 9-3

Write the command that will delete the record for Order Number 20100130.

Show the updated ORDERS table.

Solutions

Practice Exercise 9-1

```
UPDATE ORDERS
SET PRICE = 28.99
WHERE ORDERNO = 20100125;


UPDATE ORDERS
SET PRICE = 16.55
WHERE ORDERNO = 20100127;
```

```
+----------+------------+-----------+----------+-------+
| ORDERNO  | ORDERDATE  | PRODUCTID | QUANTITY | PRICE |
+----------+------------+-----------+----------+-------+
| 20100123 | 2019-09-01 |    101001 |       98 | 28.99 |
| 20100124 | 2019-09-05 |    101005 |       46 | 16.55 |
| 20100125 | 2019-09-07 |    101001 |       87 | 28.99 |
| 20100126 | 2019-09-10 |    101008 |       92 | 25.77 |
| 20100127 | 2019-09-11 |    101005 |       15 | 16.55 |
+----------+------------+-----------+----------+-------+
5 rows in set (0.03 sec)
```

Practice Exercise 9-2

```
INSERT INTO ORDERS
VALUES(20100128, 20190912, 101008, 98, 25.77);


INSERT INTO ORDERS
VALUES(20100129, 20190913, 101009, 46, 50.55);


INSERT INTO ORDERS
VALUES(20100130, 20190914, 101001, 87, 28.99);
```

INSERT INTO ORDERS

VALUES(20100131, 20190920, 101007, 92, 29.76);

INSERT INTO ORDERS

VALUES(2010032, 20190921, 101009, 15, 50.55);

```
+----------+------------+-----------+----------+-------+
| ORDERNO  | ORDERDATE  | PRODUCTID | QUANTITY | PRICE |
+----------+------------+-----------+----------+-------+
| 20100123 | 2019-09-01 |    101001 |       98 | 28.99 |
| 20100124 | 2019-09-05 |    101005 |       46 | 16.55 |
| 20100125 | 2019-09-07 |    101001 |       87 | 28.99 |
| 20100126 | 2019-09-10 |    101008 |       92 | 25.77 |
| 20100127 | 2019-09-11 |    101005 |       15 | 16.55 |
| 20100128 | 2019-09-12 |    101008 |       98 | 25.77 |
| 20100129 | 2019-09-13 |    101009 |       46 | 50.55 |
| 20100130 | 2019-09-14 |    101001 |       87 | 28.99 |
| 20100131 | 2019-09-20 |    101007 |       92 | 29.76 |
| 20100132 | 2019-09-21 |    101009 |       15 | 50.55 |
+----------+------------+-----------+----------+-------+
10 rows in set (0.01 sec)
```

Practice Exercise 9-3

DELETE FROM ORDERS

WHERE ORDERNO = 20100130;

SELECT * FROM ORDERS;

```
+----------+------------+-----------+----------+-------+
| ORDERNO  | ORDERDATE  | PRODUCTID | QUANTITY | PRICE |
+----------+------------+-----------+----------+-------+
| 20100123 | 2019-09-01 |    101001 |       98 | 28.99 |
| 20100124 | 2019-09-05 |    101005 |       46 | 16.55 |
| 20100125 | 2019-09-07 |    101001 |       87 | 28.99 |
| 20100126 | 2019-09-10 |    101008 |       92 | 25.77 |
| 20100127 | 2019-09-11 |    101005 |       15 | 16.55 |
| 20100128 | 2019-09-12 |    101008 |       98 | 25.77 |
| 20100129 | 2019-09-13 |    101009 |       46 | 50.55 |
| 20100131 | 2019-09-20 |    101007 |       92 | 29.76 |
| 20100132 | 2019-09-21 |    101009 |       15 | 50.55 |
+----------+------------+-----------+----------+-------+
9 rows in set (0.00 sec)
```

Chapter 10: Performing Subqueries

A subquery, also called Inner Query, Inner Select, or Nested Query, is a query nested within a main query and embedded within a WHERE, FROM, or SELECT clause. You will normally run a subquery to fetch data required by the main query. Hence, a subquery must be executed ahead so that its result can be passed to the primary query.

To execute a subquery, you will use comparison operators such as <, >, =. You may also use multiple row operators like ANY, ALL, BETWEEN, or IN.

You can write subqueries with the SELECT, UPDATE, INSERT, or DELETE statements to perform the following tasks:

- Check if a given expression exists in the query result.

- Compare the query result to an expression.

- Verify if the query selects a record.

There are some rules that you have to consider when using subqueries:

- Subqueries should be enclosed by parentheses.
- A subquery cannot use an ORDER BY clause because it does not have the ability to manipulate results internally. You may only use the ORDER BY clause as the last clause in the SELECT statement of the outer query. However, a subquery may use the GROUP BY clause to perform the same function.
- Subqueries, in general, can only take a single column in a SELECT clause. An exception occurs when the main query has several columns and the subquery has to compare multiple columns.
- A subquery cannot be enclosed directly in a set function.
- The SELECT list may not contain references to values that result in a BLOB, ARRAY, CLOB, or NCLOB.
- A subquery that outputs multiple rows requires multiple value operators. The IN operator is one example of multiple value operators.
- You may use the BETWEEN operator inside subqueries but it cannot be used with subqueries.
- Subqueries are written on the right side of comparison operators.

A subquery may return multiple rows and columns or a single row, which can be nested or correlated.

Subquery with the SELECT Statement

Most subqueries are written with the SELECT statement.

Here is a basic syntax:

```
SELECT column_name [, column_name ]
FROM   table1 [, table2 ]
WHERE  column_name OPERATOR
  (SELECT column_name [, column_name ]
  FROM table1 [, table2 ]
  [WHERE])
```

To demonstrate, you can use the EMPLOYEES_SALES table with the following data:

ID	INT(5) NOT NULL
AGENT	VARCHAR(40) NOT NULL
SALES	DECIMAL(9,2)
BRANCH	VARCHAR(25)
PRIMARY ID	ID

ID	AGENT	SALES	BRANCH
16015	Patricia McMilian	80,000.00	Arizona
17021	Lola Bowker	25,000.00	Utah
17024	Robert Hamson	40,000.00	Michigan
17050	Brent Ringer	20,000.00	Illinois
17088	Judy Wilson	50,000.00	Arizona
18017	Daryl Philips	30,000.00	Utah
18024	Kathleen Rivers	21,000.00	Ohio
18058	John Harrison	34,789.00	Georgia
18064	Alex Mosley	24,500.00	Illinois
18075	Greg Kendall	39,245.00	Washington
18094	Brian Martin	34,500.00	Colorado
19015	Russel Harris	26,458.00	Maryland
19023	Richard Foulks	63,589.00	Washington
19025	Susan Taylor	64,590.00	Florida
19033	James Roberson	29,874.00	South Carolina
19048	Alice Perkins	17,759.00	Michigan
19065	Michael Bourne	22,200.00	Ohio

Let us say you want to produce a report that will display the name, branches, and sales of agents with more than 35,000.00 annual sales. You can execute this statement:

SELECT AGENT, BRANCH, SALES FROM EMPLOYEE_SALES
WHERE ID IN (SELECT ID FROM EMPLOYEE_SALES
WHERE SALES > 35000.00);

Notice that the subquery specifies that only the agents whose sales exceed 35,000 should be included in the report.

Here is the result of the query:

```
+------------------------+-------------+-------------+
| AGENT                  | BRANCH      | SALES       |
+------------------------+-------------+-------------+
| Patricia McMilian      | Arizona     | 80000.00    |
| Robert Hamson          | Michigan    | 40000.00    |
| Judy Wilson            | Arizona     | 50000.00    |
| Greg Kendall           | Washington  | 39245.00    |
| Richard Foulks         | Washington  | 63589.00    |
| Susan Taylor           | Florida     | 64590.00    |
+------------------------+-------------+-------------+
6 rows in set (0.13 sec)
```

Only six agents matched the criteria defined by the subquery. You can check this manually by reviewing the table.

Subquery with the INSERT Statement

You may also perform subqueries with the INSERT statement. The data returned by a subquery will be inserted into a table.

The selected data could be modified using the date, character, or number functions.

Here is the syntax:

```
INSERT INTO table_name [ (column1 [, column2 ]) ]
   SELECT [ *|column1 [, column2 ]
   FROM table1 [, table2 ]
   [ WHERE VALUE OPERATOR ]
```

To demonstrate, you have to create a new table named AGENTSALES using the same structure as that of EMPLOYEE _SALES table:

ID	INT(5) NOT NULL
AGENT	VARCHAR(40) NOT NULL
SALES	DECIMAL(9,2)
BRANCH	VARCHAR(25)
PRIMARY KEY	ID

Instead of creating a new table from scratch, you can copy the entire content of the EMPLOYEE_SALES table to the new AGENTSALES table with the following statement:

INSERT INTO AGENTSALES

SELECT * FROM EMPLOYEE_SALES

WHERE ID IN (SELECT ID

FROM EMPLOYEE_SALES);

To view the new table:

SELECT * FROM AGENTSALES;

```
mysql> SELECT * FROM AGENTSALES;
+-------+------------------+----------+----------------+
| ID    | AGENT            | SALES    | BRANCH         |
+-------+------------------+----------+----------------+
| 16015 | Patricia McMilian| 80000.00 | Arizona        |
| 17021 | Lola Bowker      | 25000.00 | Utah           |
| 17024 | Robert Hamson    | 40000.00 | Michigan       |
| 17050 | Brent Ringer     | 20000.00 | Illinois       |
| 17088 | Judy Wilson      | 50000.00 | Arizona        |
| 18017 | Daryl Philips    | 30000.00 | Utah           |
| 18024 | Kathleen Rivers  | 21000.00 | Ohio           |
| 18058 | John Harrison    | 34789.00 | Georgia        |
| 18064 | Alex Mosley      | 24500.00 | Illinois       |
| 18075 | Greg Kendall     | 39245.00 | Washington     |
| 18094 | Brian Martin     | 34500.00 | Colorado       |
| 19015 | Russel Harris    | 26458.00 | Maryland       |
| 19023 | Richard Foulks   | 63589.00 | Washington     |
| 19025 | Susan Taylor     | 64590.00 | Florida        |
| 19033 | James Roberson   | 29874.00 | South Carolina |
| 19048 | Alice Perkins    | 17759.00 | Michigan       |
| 19065 | Michael Bourne   | 22200.00 | Ohio           |
+-------+------------------+----------+----------------+
17 rows in set (0.00 sec)
```

You now have two tables with the same structures and data.

Subquery with the UPDATE Statement

You can also perform subqueries with the UPDATE command. Executing a subquery with an UPDATE statement will result in the updating of one or more columns in a table.

Here is the basic syntax:

```
UPDATE table
SET column_name = new_value
[ WHERE OPERATOR [ VALUE ]
  (SELECT COLUMN_NAME
  FROM TABLE_NAME)
  [ WHERE) ]
```

You can use the AGENTSALES table for this example.

The following statement will update the SALES by 3x for all agents whose branch is equal to 'Arizona':

```
UPDATE AGENTSALES
  SET SALES = SALES * 3
  WHERE BRANCH IN (SELECT BRANCH FROM EMPLOYEE_SALES
    WHERE BRANCH = 'Arizona');
```

Notice that for this purpose, you have to make a reference to the EMPLOYEE_SALES table which has the same structure as AGENTSALES, the target table.

The above statement will have an impact on two rows since there are two agents in the Arizona branch.

At this point, you can run the select command to view the updated AGENTSALES table:

SELECT * FROM AGENTSALES

Here's the output:

```
+-------+------------------+-----------+----------------+
| ID    | AGENT            | SALES     | BRANCH         |
+-------+------------------+-----------+----------------+
| 16015 | Patricia McMilian| 240000.00 | Arizona        |
| 17021 | Lola Bowker      | 25000.00  | Utah           |
| 17024 | Robert Hamson    | 40000.00  | Michigan       |
| 17050 | Brent Ringer     | 20000.00  | Illinois       |
| 17088 | Judy Wilson      | 150000.00 | Arizona        |
| 18017 | Daryl Philips    | 30000.00  | Utah           |
| 18024 | Kathleen Rivers  | 21000.00  | Ohio           |
| 18058 | John Harrison    | 34789.00  | Georgia        |
| 18064 | Alex Mosley      | 24500.00  | Illinois       |
| 18075 | Greg Kendall     | 39245.00  | Washington     |
| 18094 | Brian Martin     | 34500.00  | Colorado       |
| 19015 | Russel Harris    | 26458.00  | Maryland       |
| 19023 | Richard Foulks   | 63589.00  | Washington     |
| 19025 | Susan Taylor     | 64590.00  | Florida        |
| 19033 | James Roberson   | 29874.00  | South Carolina |
| 19048 | Alice Perkins    | 17759.00  | Michigan       |
| 19065 | Michael Bourne   | 22200.00  | Ohio           |
+-------+------------------+-----------+----------------+
17 rows in set (3.63 sec)
```

Subquery with the DELETE Statement

Subqueries can also be performed using the DELETE command. This operation will delete records that match the condition.

Here's the basic syntax:

```
DELETE FROM TABLE_NAME
[ WHERE OPERATOR [ VALUE ]
  (SELECT COLUMN_NAME
  FROM TABLE_NAME)
  [ WHERE) ]
```

You can use the AGENTSALES table for this example. You will also reference the EMPLOYEE_SALES, the orginal table which has identical structures.

The following statement will delete the records of all employees with sales that are less than 30,000:

DELETE FROM AGENTSALES

WHERE SALES IN (SELECT SALES FROM EMPLOYEE_SALES

WHERE SALES < 30000.00);

The subquery operation with the DELETE statement will have an impact on eight agents whose sales are below 30,000.

The updated AGENTSALES table shows that there are only nine remaining records:

```
+-------+------------------+-----------+------------+
| ID    | AGENT            | SALES     | BRANCH     |
+-------+------------------+-----------+------------+
| 16015 | Patricia McMilian | 240000.00 | Arizona    |
| 17024 | Robert Hamson    |  40000.00 | Michigan   |
| 17088 | Judy Wilson      | 150000.00 | Arizona    |
| 18017 | Daryl Philips    |  30000.00 | Utah       |
| 18058 | John Harrison    |  34789.00 | Georgia    |
| 18075 | Greg Kendall     |  39245.00 | Washington |
| 18094 | Brian Martin     |  34500.00 | Colorado   |
| 19023 | Richard Foulks   |  63589.00 | Washington |
| 19025 | Susan Taylor     |  64590.00 | Florida    |
+-------+------------------+-----------+------------+
9 rows in set (0.00 sec)
```

Summary

Subqueries are queries nested inside a main query and are embedded in a WHERE, FROM, or SELECT clause. It is used to extract data needed by the principal query. A subquery uses comparison operators such as <, > or = and may require multiple row operators like ANY, ALL, BETWEEN, and IN.

Practice Exercises

Practice Exercise 10-1

For this exercise, you will use the ORDERS table from the DATACLASS database:

```
+----------+------------+-----------+----------+--------+
| ORDERNO  | ORDERDATE  | PRODUCTID | QUANTITY | PRICE  |
+----------+------------+-----------+----------+--------+
| 20100123 | 2019-09-01 |    101001 |       98 | 28.99  |
| 20100124 | 2019-09-05 |    101005 |       46 | 16.55  |
| 20100125 | 2019-09-07 |    101001 |       87 | 28.99  |
| 20100126 | 2019-09-10 |    101008 |       92 | 25.77  |
| 20100127 | 2019-09-11 |    101005 |       15 | 16.55  |
| 20100128 | 2019-09-12 |    101008 |       98 | 25.77  |
| 20100129 | 2019-09-13 |    101009 |       46 | 50.55  |
| 20100131 | 2019-09-20 |    101007 |       92 | 29.76  |
| 20100132 | 2019-09-21 |    101009 |       15 | 50.55  |
+----------+------------+-----------+----------+--------+
9 rows in set (0.00 sec)
```

Write a statement that will display the Order Number, Order Date, and Quantity of Orders where the quantity is more than 50.

Show the Updated ORDERS table

Solution

Practice Exercise 10-1

SELECT ORDERNO, ORDERDATE, QUANTITY FROM ORDERS
WHERE ORDERNO IN(SELECT ORDERNO FROM ORDERS)
WHERE QUANTITY > 50);

SHOW * FROM ORDERS;

```
+------------+------------+----------+
| ORDERNO    | ORDERDATE  | QUANTITY |
+------------+------------+----------+
| 20100123   | 2019-09-01 |       98 |
| 20100125   | 2019-09-07 |       87 |
| 20100126   | 2019-09-10 |       92 |
| 20100128   | 2019-09-12 |       98 |
| 20100131   | 2019-09-20 |       92 |
+------------+------------+----------+
5 rows in set (0.18 sec)
```

Chapter 11: Combining and Joining Tables

SQL is a powerful database language. It is equipped with the features and structures that allow huge organizations to maintain and operate large chunks of data. Its real strength comes from its ability to work with different sets of data at once.

Relational databases are comprised of tables that are related to each other through common values. These shared identifiers are used to combine data from several tables.

Joins are valuable features of SQL. They make data management and operations more efficient.

SQL supports several types of JOIN operations such as:

INNER JOIN
LEFT JOIN
LEFT OUTER JOIN
RIGHT JOIN
FULL OUTER JOIN

INNER JOIN

The INNER JOIN, also called EQUIJOIN or JOIN, is the most frequently used and most important type of JOINS. It is used to create a new table out of two existing tables based off the join-predicate. In this join operation, each row of the first table is compared with every row of the second table to determine the matching rows that meet the criteria of the join-predicate. An INNER JOIN eliminates rows that do not meet the JOIN condition and returns the matching pairs of rows as a new table.

Syntax:

```
SELECT table1.column1, table2.column2...
FROM table1
INNER JOIN table2
ON table1.common_field = table2.common_field;
```

To demonstrate how the INNER JOIN works, you can use the SALES table and CUSTOMERS table from the steelcompany database with the following data:

CUSTOMERS table

```
+------------+-----------------+--------------------------------------------+
| CUST_CODE  | CUSTOMER        | ADDRESS                                    |
+------------+-----------------+--------------------------------------------+
|      17432 | CYCLING ACTS    | 2330 KINNEY STREET SPRINGFIELD MA          |
|      18024 | SPIN AND TURN   | 1242 SPRING STREET ELVASTON IL             |
|      18263 | SHELL SUPPLIES  | 196 DALE AVENUE HANKAMER TX                |
|      18266 | SINCERE DAYCARE | 248 GREEN STREET SMITHVILLE TN             |
|      19111 | TOPSY TURVY CORP| 362 ROSE AVENUE NEW ORLEAS LA              |
|      19123 | BEST MAN STORE  | 3723 MIDDLEVILLE ROAD, LONG ANGELES CA     |
|      19184 | KENDRA PARKS    | 5349 FINCHAM ROAD SAN DIEGO CA             |
|      19238 | AGC MERCHANDISE | 3702 MY DRIVE WHITESTONE NY                |
|      19253 | POOLS AND PATIO | 2371 HANIFAN LANE ROSWELL GA               |
|      19435 | XYZ BUSINESS    | 3205 MARSHVILLE ROAD POUGHKEEPSKIE NY      |
+------------+-----------------+--------------------------------------------+
```

SALES table

```
+------------+-----------+-------------+-----------+-------------+
| INVOICE    | PROD_ID   | QUANTITY    | SALES     | CUST_CODE   |
+------------+-----------+-------------+-----------+-------------+
|        114 |      1020 |          24 |    444.00 |       17432 |
|        115 |      1010 |          12 |    180.00 |       19123 |
|        116 |      1020 |          43 |    795.50 |       18024 |
|        117 |      1010 |          13 |    195.00 |       19111 |
|        118 |      1010 |          25 |    375.00 |       19238 |
|        119 |      1020 |          34 |    629.00 |       19253 |
|        120 |      1020 |          48 |    888.00 |       18024 |
+------------+-----------+-------------+-----------+-------------+
```

SELECT CUSTOMERS.CUST_CODE,
CUSTOMERS.CUSTOMER, CUSTOMERS.ADDRESS

FROM CUSTOMERS

INNER JOIN SALES

ON CUSTOMERS.CUST_CODE = SALES.CUST_CODE;

Output:

```
+-----------+------------------+--------------------------------------------+
| CUST_CODE | CUSTOMER         | ADDRESS                                    |
+-----------+------------------+--------------------------------------------+
|     17432 | CYCLING ACTS     | 2330 KINNEY STREET SPRINGFIELD MA          |
|     19123 | BEST MAN STORE   | 3723 MIDDLEVILLE ROAD, LONG ANGELES CA     |
|     18024 | SPIN AND TURN    | 1242 SPRING STREET ELVASTON IL             |
|     19111 | TOPSY TURVY CORP | 362 ROSE AVENUE NEW ORLEAS LA              |
|     19238 | AGC MERCHANDISE  | 3702 MY DRIVE WHITESTONE NY                |
|     19253 | POOLS AND PATIO  | 2371 HANIFAN LANE ROSWELL GA               |
|     18024 | SPIN AND TURN    | 1242 SPRING STREET ELVASTON IL             |
+-----------+------------------+--------------------------------------------+
7 rows in set (0.13 sec)
```

The query returned a table with 7 rows showing the customer code, customer name, and address of the customers listed in the CUSTOMERS table with matching record in the SALES table.

Alternatively, you can use the following simple statement to carry out a JOIN operation:

SELECT CUST_CODE, CUSTOMER, ADDRESS

FROM CUSTOMERS

JOIN SALES USING(CUST_CODE);

The above statement uses the USING clause, which results in a much simpler statement for the JOIN operation. It returns a similar output:

```
mysql> SELECT CUST_CODE, CUSTOMER, ADDRESS FROM CUSTOMERS
    -> JOIN SALES USING(CUST_CODE);
+-----------+----------------+------------------------------------+
| CUST_CODE | CUSTOMER       | ADDRESS                            |
+-----------+----------------+------------------------------------+
|     17432 | CYCLING ACTS   | 2330 KINNEY STREET SPRINGFIELD MA  |
|     19123 | BEST MAN STORE | 3723 MIDDLEVILLE ROAD, LONG ANGELES CA |
|     18024 | SPIN AND TURN  | 1242 SPRING STREET ELVASTON IL    |
|     19111 | TOPSY TURVY CORP | 362 ROSE AVENUE NEW ORLEAS LA   |
|     19238 | AGC MERCHANDISE | 3702 MY DRIVE WHITESTONE NY      |
|     19253 | POOLS AND PATIO | 2371 HANIFAN LANE ROSWELL GA    |
|     18024 | SPIN AND TURN  | 1242 SPRING STREET ELVASTON IL    |
+-----------+----------------+------------------------------------+
7 rows in set (0.00 sec)
```

You can also perform a join operation by using an alias name for your column when you execute a SELECT statement.

Here is the statement:

SELECT   a.CUST_CODE,   b.CUST_CODE,   CUSTOMER,
ADDRESS
FROM CUSTOMERS AS a
JOIN SALES as b ON a.CUST_CODE = b.CUST_CODE;

Output:

```
mysql> SELECT a.CUST_CODE, b.CUST_CODE, CUSTOMER, ADDRESS
    -> FROM CUSTOMERS AS a
    -> JOIN SALES as b ON a.CUST_CODE = b.CUST_CODE;
+-----------+-----------+-----------------+--------------------------------------+
| CUST_CODE | CUST_CODE | CUSTOMER        | ADDRESS                              |
+-----------+-----------+-----------------+--------------------------------------+
|     17432 |     17432 | CYCLING ACTS    | 2330 KINNEY STREET SPRINGFIELD MA    |
|     19123 |     19123 | BEST MAN STORE  | 3723 MIDDLEVILLE ROAD, LONG ANGELES CA |
|     18024 |     18024 | SPIN AND TURN   | 1242 SPRING STREET ELVASTON IL      |
|     19111 |     19111 | TOPSY TURVY CORP| 362 ROSE AVENUE NEW ORLEAS LA       |
|     19238 |     19238 | AGC MERCHANDISE | 3702 MY DRIVE WHITESTONE NY         |
|     19253 |     19253 | POOLS AND PATIO | 2371 HANIFAN LANE ROSWELL GA        |
|     18024 |     18024 | SPIN AND TURN   | 1242 SPRING STREET ELVASTON IL      |
+-----------+-----------+-----------------+--------------------------------------+
7 rows in set (0.10 sec)
```

Table aliasing is the practice of using a temporary name for a table column. Using aliases for the table and table columns helps make the statements and the output more readable.

LEFT JOIN

The LEFT JOIN is used to return all rows found in the left table as well as matching records from the right table. The right table returns NULL if there are no matching values.

Syntax:

SELECT table1.column1, table2.column2...
FROM table1
LEFT JOIN table2
ON table1.common_field = table2.common_field;

To demonstrate the LEFT JOIN operation, you will use the CUSTOMERS table and SALES table from the steelcompany database with these data:

CUSTOMERS table

CUST_CODE	CUSTOMER	ADDRESS
17432	CYCLING ACTS	2330 KINNEY STREET SPRINGFIELD MA
18024	SPIN AND TURN	1242 SPRING STREET ELVASTON IL
18263	SHELL SUPPLIES	196 DALE AVENUE HANKAMER TX
18266	SINCERE DAYCARE	248 GREEN STREET SMITHVILLE TN
19111	TOPSY TURVY CORP	362 ROSE AVENUE NEW ORLEAS LA
19123	BEST MAN STORE	3723 MIDDLEVILLE ROAD, LONG ANGELES CA
19184	KENDRA PARKS	5349 FINCHAM ROAD SAN DIEGO CA
19238	AGC MERCHANDISE	3702 MY DRIVE WHITESTONE NY
19253	POOLS AND PATIO	2371 HANIFAN LANE ROSWELL GA
19435	XYZ BUSINESS	3205 MARSHVILLE ROAD POUGHKEEPSKIE NY

SALES table

```
+-----------+----------+-----------+---------+-----------+
| INVOICE   | PROD_ID  | QUANTITY  | SALES   | CUST_CODE |
+-----------+----------+-----------+---------+-----------+
|       114 |     1020 |        24 | 444.00  |     17432 |
|       115 |     1010 |        12 | 180.00  |     19123 |
|       116 |     1020 |        43 | 795.50  |     18024 |
|       117 |     1010 |        13 | 195.00  |     19111 |
|       118 |     1010 |        25 | 375.00  |     19238 |
|       119 |     1020 |        34 | 629.00  |     19253 |
|       120 |     1020 |        48 | 888.00  |     18024 |
+-----------+----------+-----------+---------+-----------+
```

To perform a LEFT JOIN operation on the CUSTOMERS table and SALES table, you can use this statement:

SELECT   CUSTOMERS.CUST_CODE,
CUSTOMERS.CUSTOMER,
    CUSTOMERS.ADDRESS,   SALES.QUANTITY,
SALES.SALES
FROM CUSTOMERS
LEFT JOIN SALES
ON CUSTOMERS.CUST_CODE = SALES.CUST_CODE;

Output:

```
+----------+----------------+--------------------------------------+----------+--------+
| CUST_CODE | CUSTOMER      | ADDRESS                              | QUANTITY | SALES  |
+----------+----------------+--------------------------------------+----------+--------+
|    17432 | CYCLING ACTS   | 2330 KINNEY STREET SPRINGFIELD MA    |       24 | 444.00 |
|    19123 | BEST MAN STORE | 3723 MIDDLEVILLE ROAD, LONG ANGELES CA |     12 | 180.00 |
|    18024 | SPIN AND TURN  | 1242 SPRING STREET ELVASTON IL       |       43 | 795.50 |
|    19111 | TOPSY TURVY CORP | 362 ROSE AVENUE NEW ORLEAS LA      |       13 | 195.00 |
|    19238 | AGC MERCHANDISE | 3702 MY DRIVE WHITESTONE NY         |       25 | 375.00 |
|    19253 | POOLS AND PATIO | 2371 HANIFAN LANE ROSWELL GA        |       34 | 629.00 |
|    18024 | SPIN AND TURN  | 1242 SPRING STREET ELVASTON IL       |       48 | 888.00 |
|    18263 | SHELL SUPPLIES | 196 DALE AVENUE HANKAMER TX          |     NULL |   NULL |
|    18266 | SINCERE DAYCARE | 248 GREEN STREET SMITHVILLE TN      |     NULL |   NULL |
|    19184 | KENDRA PARKS   | 5349 FINCHAM ROAD SAN DIEGO CA       |     NULL |   NULL |
|    19435 | XYZ BUSINESS   | 3205 MARSHVILLE ROAD POUGHKEEPSKIE NY |    NULL |   NULL |
+----------+----------------+--------------------------------------+----------+--------+
11 rows in set (0.06 sec)
```

The SELECT statement above returned a new table showing the CUST_CODE, which is the common field between the CUSTOMERS table and the SALES table, the CUSTOMER and ADDRESS column from the CUSTOMERS table, and the QUANTITY and SALES columns from the SALES table.

Take note that with the LEFT JOIN operation, the SELECT query returned NULL when the SALES table columns (QUANTITY and SALES) have no matching values for the records in the CUSTOMERS table columns.

RIGHT JOIN

The RIGHT JOIN is used to return all rows in the right table as well as matching records from the left table. The left table returns NULL if there are no matching values.

Syntax:

```
SELECT table1.column1, table2.column2…
FROM table1
RIGHT JOIN table2
ON table1.common_field = table2.common_field;
```

To demonstrate the RIGHT JOIN operation, you will use the CUSTOMERS table and SALES table from the steelcompany database with these data:

CUSTOMERS table

```
+----------+-------------------+------------------------------------------+
| CUST_CODE | CUSTOMER          | ADDRESS                                   |
+----------+-------------------+------------------------------------------+
|    17432 | CYCLING ACTS      | 2330 KINNEY STREET SPRINGFIELD MA         |
|    18024 | SPIN AND TURN     | 1242 SPRING STREET ELVASTON IL            |
|    18263 | SHELL SUPPLIES    | 196 DALE AVENUE HANKAMER TX               |
|    18266 | SINCERE DAYCARE   | 248 GREEN STREET SMITHVILLE TN            |
|    19111 | TOPSY TURVY CORP  | 362 ROSE AVENUE NEW ORLEAS LA             |
|    19123 | BEST MAN STORE    | 3723 MIDDLEVILLE ROAD, LONG ANGELES CA    |
|    19184 | KENDRA PARKS      | 5349 FINCHAM ROAD SAN DIEGO CA            |
|    19238 | AGC MERCHANDISE   | 3702 MY DRIVE WHITESTONE NY               |
|    19253 | POOLS AND PATIO   | 2371 HANIFAN LANE ROSWELL GA              |
|    19435 | XYZ BUSINESS      | 3205 MARSHVILLE ROAD POUGHKEEPSKIE NY     |
+----------+-------------------+------------------------------------------+
```

SALES table

```
+-----------+----------+-----------+----------+-----------+
| INVOICE   | PROD_ID  | QUANTITY  | SALES    | CUST_CODE |
+-----------+----------+-----------+----------+-----------+
|       114 |     1020 |        24 |  444.00  |     17432 |
|       115 |     1010 |        12 |  180.00  |     19123 |
|       116 |     1020 |        43 |  795.50  |     18024 |
|       117 |     1010 |        13 |  195.00  |     19111 |
|       118 |     1010 |        25 |  375.00  |     19238 |
|       119 |     1020 |        34 |  629.00  |     19253 |
|       120 |     1020 |        48 |  888.00  |     18024 |
+-----------+----------+-----------+----------+-----------+
```

To perform a RIGHT JOIN operation on the CUSTOMERS table and SALES table, you will use this statement:

SELECT   CUSTOMERS.CUST_CODE,
CUSTOMERS.CUSTOMER,
      CUSTOMERS.ADDRESS,   SALES.QUANTITY,
SALES.SALES
FROM CUSTOMERS
RIGHT JOIN SALES
ON CUSTOMERS.CUST_CODE = SALES.CUST_CODE;

Output:

```
+----------+----------------+---------------------------------------+----------+--------+
| CUST_CODE | CUSTOMER      | ADDRESS                               | QUANTITY | SALES  |
+----------+----------------+---------------------------------------+----------+--------+
|    17432 | CYCLING ACTS   | 2330 KINNEY STREET SPRINGFIELD MA     |       24 | 444.00 |
|    19123 | BEST MAN STORE | 3723 MIDDLEVILLE ROAD, LONG ANGELES CA |      12 | 180.00 |
|    18024 | SPIN AND TURN  | 1242 SPRING STREET ELVASTON IL        |       43 | 795.50 |
|    19111 | TOPSY TURVY CORP | 362 ROSE AVENUE NEW ORLEAS LA       |       13 | 195.00 |
|    19238 | AGC MERCHANDISE | 3702 MY DRIVE WHITESTONE NY          |       25 | 375.00 |
|    19253 | POOLS AND PATIO | 2371 HANIFAN LANE ROSWELL GA         |       34 | 629.00 |
|    18024 | SPIN AND TURN  | 1242 SPRING STREET ELVASTON IL        |       48 | 888.00 |
+----------+----------------+---------------------------------------+----------+--------+
7 rows in set (0.19 sec)
```

The SELECT statement above returned a new table showing the CUST_CODE, which is the common field between the CUSTOMERS table and the SALES table, the CUSTOMER and ADDRESS column from the CUSTOMERS table, and the QUANTITY and SALES columns from the SALES table.

Notice that unlike the LEFT JOIN operation, which returned 11 rows of data, the RIGHT JOIN operation returned 7 rows of data. The number of records shown in the result table corresponds to the number of rows in the SALES table, which is the right table. Since all records in the SALES table have matching records in the CUSTOMERS table, the new table did not return a NULL value.

FULL JOIN

The FULL JOIN operation is used to display the combined results of the LEFT and RIGHT JOINS. The resulting table contains all data from the tables returned by both JOIN operations. If there are missing matches, it returns NULL values.

Syntax:

```
SELECT table1.column1, table2.column2...
FROM table1
FULL JOIN table2
ON table1.common_field = table2.common_field;
```

Summary

The ability to bring different sets of data together at once is one of the most powerful features of SQL. Relational databases use common identifiers that make it possible to combine data from multiple tables. SQL supports several JOIN operations that you can use to retrieve more meaningful and useful reports from your database.

Practice Exercises

Practice Exercise 11-1

For this exercise, you will use the PRODUCTS table and the ORDERS table from the CLASSDATA database.

Products Table

PRODUCTID	PRODNAME	PRICE	INSTOCK	ONORDER
101001	Butterfly Hinge 1	28.99	25	185
101002	Butterfly Hinge 2	32.44	30	0
101003	White Glue .5L	15.65	876	0
101004	White Glue 1L	28.99	874	0
101005	Drawer Runner .5	16.55	15	61
101006	Drawer Runner 1	30.27	410	0
101007	Deco Applique A	29.76	132	0
101008	Deco Applique B	25.77	212	92
101009	MDF Sheet	50.55	543	0
101010	Wood Frame	70.14	202	0

Orders Table

```
+----------+------------+-----------+----------+--------+
| ORDERNO  | ORDERDATE  | PRODUCTID | QUANTITY | PRICE  |
+----------+------------+-----------+----------+--------+
| 20100123 | 2019-09-01 |   101001  |       98 | 28.99  |
| 20100124 | 2019-09-05 |   101005  |       46 | 16.55  |
| 20100125 | 2019-09-07 |   101001  |       87 | 28.99  |
| 20100126 | 2019-09-10 |   101008  |       92 | 25.77  |
| 20100127 | 2019-09-11 |   101005  |       15 | 16.55  |
| 20100128 | 2019-09-12 |   101008  |       98 | 25.77  |
| 20100129 | 2019-09-13 |   101009  |       46 | 50.55  |
| 20100131 | 2019-09-20 |   101007  |       92 | 29.76  |
| 20100132 | 2019-09-21 |   101009  |       15 | 50.55  |
+----------+------------+-----------+----------+--------+
```

Write a statement that will show the Product ID, Product Name, and Price of Products, which have corresponding records in the ORDERS table.

Show the result of the query.

Exercise 11-2

This exercise will use the PRODUCTS table and ORDERS table.

Write a statement that will show the Product ID, Product Name, Order Number, Order Date, and Quantity Ordered for products listed in the ORDERS table.

Show the result.

Solution

Practice 11-1

SELECT PRODUCTS.PRODUCTID, PRODUCTS.PRODNAME,
PRODUCTS.PRICE
FROM PRODUCTS
INNER JOIN ORDERS
ON PRODUCTS.PRODUCTID = ORDERS.PRODUCTID;

Output:

```
+-----------+----------------------+--------+
| PRODUCTID | PRODNAME             | PRICE  |
+-----------+----------------------+--------+
|    101001 | Butterfly Hinge 1    | 28.99  |
|    101005 | Drawer Runner  .5    | 16.55  |
|    101001 | Butterfly Hinge 1    | 28.99  |
|    101008 | Deco Applique B      | 25.77  |
|    101005 | Drawer Runner  .5    | 16.55  |
|    101008 | Deco Applique B      | 25.77  |
|    101009 | MDF Sheet            | 50.55  |
|    101007 | Deco Applique A      | 29.76  |
|    101009 | MDF Sheet            | 50.55  |
+-----------+----------------------+--------+
9 rows in set (0.00 sec)
```

Practice Exercise 11-2

SELECT PRODUCTS.PRODUCTID, PRODUCTS.PRODNAME,

ORDERS.ORDERNO, ORDERS.ORDERDATE,

ORDER.QUANTITY

FROM PRODUCTS

RIGHT JOIN ORDERS

ON PRODUCTS.PRODUCTID = ORDERS.PRODUCTID;

Output:

```
+-----------+--------------------+----------+------------+----------+
| PRODUCTID | PRODNAME           | ORDERNO  | ORDERDATE  | QUANTITY |
+-----------+--------------------+----------+------------+----------+
|    101001 | Butterfly Hinge 1  | 20100123 | 2019-09-01 |       98 |
|    101005 | Drawer Runner .5   | 20100124 | 2019-09-05 |       46 |
|    101001 | Butterfly Hinge 1  | 20100125 | 2019-09-07 |       87 |
|    101008 | Deco Applique B    | 20100126 | 2019-09-10 |       92 |
|    101005 | Drawer Runner .5   | 20100127 | 2019-09-11 |       15 |
|    101008 | Deco Applique B    | 20100128 | 2019-09-12 |       98 |
|    101009 | MDF Sheet          | 20100129 | 2019-09-13 |       46 |
|    101007 | Deco Applique A    | 20100131 | 2019-09-20 |       92 |
|    101009 | MDF Sheet          | 20100132 | 2019-09-21 |       15 |
+-----------+--------------------+----------+------------+----------+
9 rows in set (0.03 sec)
```

Chapter 12: SQL Operators

An operator is a designated word or special character that defines a condition or links one or multiple conditions in an SQL statement. SQL supports a great range of operators to enable arithmetic, comparison, and logical operation.

Operators are primarily required in the WHERE clause.

In this chapter, you will learn about the different SQL operators and see some examples of their usage.

Arithmetic Operators

+	Addition: Adds left and right operands
-	Subtraction: Subtracts right number from the left number
*	Multiplication: Multiplies the left and right operands
/	Division: Divides the left value by the right value
%	Modulus: Divides the left value by the right value and returns the remainder

Arithmetic operators work on numeric values. You will find them useful when working with real life databases that contain numeric data like sales, costs, salary, expenses, fees, etc. In this section, you will work with new tables and use arithmetic operators to extract and manipulate data.

Addition (+)

To demonstrate, you will have to create a new table, ANNUAL_REPORT, with the following specifications:

PRODUCT ID   INT(4) NOT NULL

VOLUME   INT(9)

TOTAL_COST   DECIMAL(10,2)

TOTAL_SALES   DECIMAL(10,2)

The ANNUAL_REPORT table contains the following data:

PRODUCT_ID	VOLUME	TOTAL_COST	TOTAL_SALES
1010	34,500	86,250.00	103,500.00
1020	12,066	28,958.40	37,645.92
2010	67,234	161,361.60	201,702.00
2020	11,066	25,451.80	31,814.75
3010	23,098	53,125.40	64,812.99
3030	22,472	47,191.20	60,404.74
4010	9,876	20,739.60	37,331.28
4020	1,254	2,658.48	4,253.57
5010	46,987	84,576.60	105,720.75
5020	24,926	55,086.46	70,510.67

```
+------------+---------+------------+-------------+
| PRODUCT_ID | VOLUME  | TOTAL_COST | TOTAL_SALES |
+------------+---------+------------+-------------+
|       1010 |   34500 |   86250.00 |   103500.00 |
|       1020 |   12066 |   28958.40 |    37645.92 |
|       2010 |   67234 |  161361.60 |   201702.00 |
|       2020 |   11066 |   25451.80 |    31814.75 |
|       3010 |   23098 |   53125.40 |    64812.99 |
|       3030 |   22472 |   47191.20 |    60404.74 |
|       4010 |    9876 |   20739.60 |    37331.28 |
|       4020 |    1254 |    2658.48 |     4253.57 |
|       5010 |   46987 |   84576.60 |   105720.75 |
|       5020 |   24926 |   55086.46 |    70510.67 |
+------------+---------+------------+-------------+
10 rows in set (0.11 sec)
```

Let us say you want to display the products with a combined TOTAL_COST and TOTAL_SALES value, which is more than 80,000, you can execute this statement:

SELECT PRODUCT_ID, TOTAL_COST, TOTAL_SALES
FROM ANNUAL_REPORT
WHERE (TOTAL_COST + TOTAL_SALES) > 80000;

Here is the output:

```
+--------------+---------------+---------------+
| PRODUCT_ID   | TOTAL_COST    | TOTAL_SALES   |
+--------------+---------------+---------------+
|       1010   |    86250.00   |    103500.00  |
|       2010   |   161361.60   |    201702.00  |
|       3010   |    53125.40   |     64812.99  |
|       3030   |    47191.20   |     60404.74  |
|       5010   |    84576.60   |    105720.75  |
|       5020   |    55086.46   |     70510.67  |
+--------------+---------------+---------------+
```

Only 6 records out of 10 satisfied the criteria.

You can also use the addition operator directly on the table data using a random number. For example, to add 1,000 to the volume data of Product ID 5020, you can use this statement:

SELECT VOLUME + 1000
FROM ANNUAL_REPORT
WHERE PRODUCT_ID = 5020;

Here is the output:

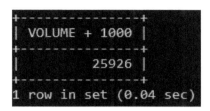

Subtraction (-)

You will be using the same table, ANNUAL_REPORT, to demonstrate how the subtraction operation is used in SQL.

Assuming you want to display the products with a net margin (TOTAL_SALES – TOTAL_COST) of more than 20,000, here is how you will write the statement:

SELECT PRODUCT_ID, TOTAL_SALES, TOTAL_COST

FROM ANNUAL_REPORT

WHERE (TOTAL_SALES - TOTAL_COST) > 20000;

Here is the result:

```
+-------------+---------------+-------------+
| PRODUCT_ID  | TOTAL_SALES   | TOTAL_COST  |
+-------------+---------------+-------------+
|        2010 |     201702.00 |   161361.60 |
|        5010 |     105720.75 |    84576.60 |
+-------------+---------------+-------------+
2 rows in set (0.06 sec)
```

Notice that only 2 out of 10 products satisfied the criteria. Additionally, since you specified the TOTAL_SALES before the TOTAL_COST in the SELECT clause, the TOTAL_SALES column was displayed before the TOTAL_COST.

You may also apply the subtraction operation on a table data using a random number. For instance, you may want to deduct the 5,000 from the volume of Product ID 3010. You can use the following statement:

SELECT VOLUME – 5000
FROM ANNUAL_REPORT
WHERE PRODUCT_ID = 3010

Below is a screenshot of the output:

```
+-----------------+
| VOLUME - 5000 |
+-----------------+
|           18098 |
+-----------------+
1 row in set (0.03 sec)
```

Multiplication (*)

You will use the table ANNUAL_REPORT to show how the Multiplication operator (*) is used in SQL.

Let us say you need to view the products with the volume x sales value which is less than 10,000,000 and you only want to see the columns PRODUCT_ID, VOLUME, and TOTAL_SALES, you can write this statement:

SELECT PRODUCT_ID, VOLUME, TOTAL_SALES
FROM ANNUAL_REPORT
WHERE (VOLUME * TOTAL_SALES) < 10000000;

Output:

```
+--------------+----------+---------------+
| PRODUCT_ID   | VOLUME   | TOTAL_SALES   |
+--------------+----------+---------------+
|         4020 |     1254 |       4253.57 |
+--------------+----------+---------------+
1 row in set (0.00 sec)
```

Only one product satisfied the condition.

You may also use the multiplication operator on a table data with a random number as multiplier. For instance, you may want to multiple the TOTAL_SALES of Product ID No. 4020 by 1.5. You can use the following statement:

SELECT TOTAL_SALES * 1.5
FROM ANNUAL_REPORT
WHERE PRODUCT_ID = 4020;

Here is the output:

```
+-------------------+
| TOTAL_SALES * 1.5 |
+-------------------+
|          6380.355 |
+-------------------+
1 row in set (0.17 sec)
```

You can verify this by multiplying 4,253.57, the TOTAL_SALES value of Product ID 4020, by 1.5.

Division (/)

The slash (/) symbol is used to perform division operation in SQL. In this example, the ANNUAL_REPORT table will be used to show how you can use the division operator to produce a report.

Assuming that you want to display the products with average net margin per unit of more than .60, you will write this statement:

SELECT PRODUCT_ID, VOLUME, TOTAL_SALES, TOTAL_COST

FROM ANNUAL_REPORT

WHERE ((TOTAL_SALES / VOLUME) – (TOTAL_COST / VOLUME)) > .60;

This example is a little bit more complicated than the preceding ones. To get the average sales per unit, you have to divide the TOTAL_SALES by the volume. To get the average cost per unit, you have to divide the TOTAL_COST by the volume. The net margin is the difference between the average sales per unit and the average cost per unit of the product.

The output shows that there are 4 products that satisfy the specification:

```
+--------------+----------+--------------+
| PRODUCT_ID   | VOLUME   | TOTAL_SALES  |
+--------------+----------+--------------+
|        1020  |   12066  |    37645.92  |
|        4010  |    9876  |    37331.28  |
|        4020  |    1254  |     4253.57  |
|        5020  |   24926  |    70510.67  |
+--------------+----------+--------------+
4 rows in set (0.00 sec)
```

You can also use the division operator on a table data with a random number as divisor. For example, you may want to divide the TOTAL_COST of Product ID 3030 by 30. You will use the following statement or this purpose:

SELECT TOTAL_COST / 30
FROM ANNUAL_REPORT
WHERE PRODUCT_ID = 3030;

Here is the result:

```
+------------------+
| TOTAL_COST / 30  |
+------------------+
|      1573.040000 |
+------------------+
1 row in set (0.02 sec)
```

You can check the result by dividing 47,191.20, the TOTAL_COST OF Product ID 3030, by 30.

Modulos %

The modulos % operator is used to return the remainder of a division operation.

To see how this arithmetic operation can be used in SQL, you will use the ANNUAL_REPORT once more.

The modulus operator can be used as part of an expression just like the other arithmetic operations.

It can also be used with SELECT to extract data from the table and specify a modulus operation with a random number. For example, if you only want to extract the remainder of a division operation on the sales volume by 10 for Product ID No. 1020, you can write this statement:

SELECT VOLUME % 10
FROM ANNUAL_REPORT
WHERE PRODUCT_ID = 1020

This is the output:

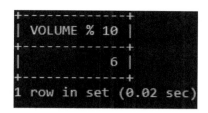

```
+--------------+
| VOLUME % 10  |
+--------------+
|            6 |
+--------------+
1 row in set (0.02 sec)
```

Comparison Operators

Relational or comparison operators are mathematical symbols, which are used to compare one expression to another. A comparison operation can return UNKNOWN, TRUE, or FALSE.

SQL supports these relational operators:

Operator	Description
=	Checks if the left and right values are equal

!=	Checks if the left and right values are not equal
<>	Checks of the left and right values are equal or not equal
>	Checks if the left value is greater than the right value
<	Checks if the left value is less than the right value
>=	Checks if the left value is greater than or equal to the right value
<=	Checks if the left value is less than or equal to the right value
!<	Checks if the left value is not less than the right value
!>	Checks if the left value is not greater than the right value

To demonstrate the usage of comparison operators in SQL, we will be using the EMPLOYEE'S table with the following data:

```
+--------+-------------------+-----------+----------------+
| ID     | AGENT             | SALES     | BRANCH         |
+--------+-------------------+-----------+----------------+
| 16015  | Patricia McMilian | 80000.00  | Arizona        |
| 17021  | Lola Bowker       | 25000.00  | Utah           |
| 17024  | Robert Hamson     | 40000.00  | Michigan       |
| 17050  | Brent Ringer      | 20000.00  | Illinois       |
| 17088  | Judy Wilson       | 50000.00  | Arizona        |
| 18017  | Daryl Philips     | 30000.00  | Utah           |
| 18024  | Kathleen Rivers   | 21000.00  | Ohio           |
| 18058  | John Harrison     | 34789.00  | Georgia        |
| 18064  | Alex Mosley       | 24500.00  | Illinois       |
| 18075  | Greg Kendall      | 39245.00  | Washington     |
| 18094  | Brian Martin      | 34500.00  | Colorado       |
| 19015  | Russel Harris     | 26458.00  | Maryland       |
| 19023  | Richard Foulks    | 63589.00  | Washington     |
| 19025  | Susan Taylor      | 64590.00  | Florida        |
| 19033  | James Roberson    | 29874.00  | South Carolina |
| 19048  | Alice Perkins     | 17759.00  | Michigan       |
| 19065  | Michael Bourne    | 22200.00  | Ohio           |
+--------+-------------------+-----------+----------------+
17 rows in set (0.84 sec)
```

The following are examples of statements that you can write to extract data from the EMPLOYEE_SALES table.

You want to view the names and sales figures of agents from Illinois:

SELECT AGENT, SALES FROM EMPLOYEE_SALES
WHERE BRANCH = 'Illinois';

Result:

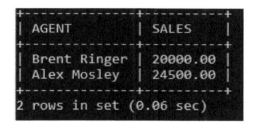

The query returned two rows of data showing the Agent's name and sales value.

You want to display all data about the agents whose sales are equal to or more than 50,000:

SELECT * FROM EMPLOYEE_SALES
WHERE SALES >= 50000.00;

Result:

```
+-------+-------------------+----------+------------+
| ID    | AGENT             | SALES    | BRANCH     |
+-------+-------------------+----------+------------+
| 16015 | Patricia McMilian | 80000.00 | Arizona    |
| 17088 | Judy Wilson       | 50000.00 | Arizona    |
| 19023 | Richard Foulks    | 63589.00 | Washington |
| 19025 | Susan Taylor      | 64590.00 | Florida    |
+-------+-------------------+----------+------------+
4 rows in set (0.02 sec)
```

The query returned four rows of data showing all column data
for Agents whose sales are equal to or more than 50,000.00.

You want to display all data on agents whose sales are not equal
to 50,000.00:

SELECT * FROM EMPLOYEE_SALES
WHERE SALES <> 50000.00;

Result:

```
+--------+----------------------+------------+-----------------+
| ID     | AGENT                | SALES      | BRANCH          |
+--------+----------------------+------------+-----------------+
| 16015  | Patricia McMilian    | 80000.00   | Arizona         |
| 17021  | Lola Bowker          | 25000.00   | Utah            |
| 17024  | Robert Hamson        | 40000.00   | Michigan        |
| 17050  | Brent Ringer         | 20000.00   | Illinois        |
| 18017  | Daryl Philips        | 30000.00   | Utah            |
| 18024  | Kathleen Rivers      | 21000.00   | Ohio            |
| 18058  | John Harrison        | 34789.00   | Georgia         |
| 18064  | Alex Mosley          | 24500.00   | Illinois        |
| 18075  | Greg Kendall         | 39245.00   | Washington      |
| 18094  | Brian Martin         | 34500.00   | Colorado        |
| 19015  | Russel Harris        | 26458.00   | Maryland        |
| 19023  | Richard Foulks       | 63589.00   | Washington      |
| 19025  | Susan Taylor         | 64590.00   | Florida         |
| 19033  | James Roberson       | 29874.00   | South Carolina  |
| 19048  | Alice Perkins        | 17759.00   | Michigan        |
| 19065  | Michael Bourne       | 22200.00   | Ohio            |
+--------+----------------------+------------+-----------------+
16 rows in set (0.03 sec)
```

The query returned 16 rows of data showing all column values for Agents whose sales are not equal to 50,000.00.

Logical Operators

Logical operators are used to compare two conditions and verify if a row can be displayed as output. In SQL, these operators compare one or more expressions and return the result.

SQL supports the following logical operators:

ANY	The ANY operator is used to compare a value to every value in the query results.
ALL	The ALL operator is used to compare a value to all values of a different set.
AND	The AND operator is used to facilitate multiple conditions in the WHERE clause of an SQL statement.
BETWEEN	The BETWEEN operator searches for value(s) within the minimum and maximum values specified.
LIKE	The LIKE operator uses wildcard operators to compare similar values.
EXISTS	The EXISTS operator searches for a row which meets a given condition.
OR	The OR operator is used to enable multiple conditions in the WHERE clause of SQL statements.
IS NULL	The IS NULL operator is used to compare one value to a NULL value.
DISTINCT	The DISTINCT operator is used to search all rows for uniqueness.
IN	The IN operator is used to compare a value to a specified range or list of literal values.
NOT	The NOT operator is used to negate the operation of the specified logical operator.

Many examples in this section will use the EMPLOYEE_SALES table with the following data:

```
+--------+------------------+-----------+-----------------+
| ID     | AGENT            | SALES     | BRANCH          |
+--------+------------------+-----------+-----------------+
| 16015  | Patricia McMilian | 80000.00 | Arizona         |
| 17021  | Lola Bowker      | 25000.00  | Utah            |
| 17024  | Robert Hamson    | 40000.00  | Michigan        |
| 17050  | Brent Ringer     | 20000.00  | Illinois        |
| 18017  | Daryl Philips    | 30000.00  | Utah            |
| 18024  | Kathleen Rivers  | 21000.00  | Ohio            |
| 18058  | John Harrison    | 34789.00  | Georgia         |
| 18064  | Alex Mosley      | 24500.00  | Illinois        |
| 18075  | Greg Kendall     | 39245.00  | Washington      |
| 18094  | Brian Martin     | 34500.00  | Colorado        |
| 19015  | Russel Harris    | 26458.00  | Maryland        |
| 19023  | Richard Foulks   | 63589.00  | Washington      |
| 19025  | Susan Taylor     | 64590.00  | Florida         |
| 19033  | James Roberson   | 29874.00  | South Carolina  |
| 19048  | Alice Perkins    | 17759.00  | Michigan        |
| 19065  | Michael Bourne   | 22200.00  | Ohio            |
+--------+------------------+-----------+-----------------+
16 rows in set (0.03 sec)
```

In addition, we will be using the EMPLOYEE_RECORD table, which contains the salary record of the agents listed in the EMPLOYEE_SALES table. These two tables share 3 common columns and data: ID, AGENT, and BRANCH.

The AND Operator

The AND Operator is used if you want to select rows that satisfy all specified conditions. It is used in the WHERE clause.

Example:

SELECT * FROM EMPLOYEE_SALES WHERE BRANCH = 'Arizona' AND SALES > 50000.00;

Only one agent matched both conditions:

```
+--------+--------------------+----------+---------+
| ID     | AGENT              | SALES    | BRANCH  |
+--------+--------------------+----------+---------+
| 16015  | Patricia McMilian  | 80000.00 | Arizona |
+--------+--------------------+----------+---------+
1 row in set (0.06 sec)
```

The OR Operator

The OR Operator allows multiple conditions. You can use this operator if you want to select rows that comply with at least one of the conditions.

Example:

SELECT * FROM EMPLOYEE_SALES
WHERE BRANCH = 'Georgia' OR SALES = 30000.00;

The query returned two rows. One row meets the BRANCH condition while the other row meets the SALES condition:

```
+-------+----------------+----------+---------+
| ID    | AGENT          | SALES    | BRANCH  |
+-------+----------------+----------+---------+
| 18017 | Daryl Philips  | 30000.00 | Utah    |
| 18058 | John Harrison  | 34789.00 | Georgia |
+-------+----------------+----------+---------+
2 rows in set (3.81 sec)
```

The NOT Operator:

The NOT operator is used to return rows that do not meet a condition. In effect, it produces the opposite result of the given condition.

For instance, if you want to identify the agents whose sales are not higher than 35,000.00, you would write a query like this:

SELECT AGENT, SALES FROM EMPLOYEE_SALES
WHERE NOT SALES > 35000.00;

The query returned 11 rows of results for agents whose sales did not exceed 35,000:

```
+-------------------+------------+
| AGENT             | SALES      |
+-------------------+------------+
| Lola Bowker       | 25000.00   |
| Brent Ringer      | 20000.00   |
| Daryl Philips     | 30000.00   |
| Kathleen Rivers   | 21000.00   |
| John Harrison     | 34789.00   |
| Alex Mosley       | 24500.00   |
| Brian Martin      | 34500.00   |
| Russel Harris     | 26458.00   |
| James Roberson    | 29874.00   |
| Alice Perkins     | 17759.00   |
| Michael Bourne    | 22200.00   |
+-------------------+------------+
11 rows in set (0.13 sec)
```

The IN Operator

This operator is a comparison keyword that you can use to compare a value to several values.

Let us say you want to determine the agents who are assigned to either Arizona or Illinois, you may launch this query statement:

SELECT ID, AGENT, BRANCH FROM EMPLOYEE_SALES
WHERE BRANCH IN ('Arizona', 'Illinois');

The database engine returned four rows of results that match the condition:

```
+-------+-------------------+------------+
| ID    | AGENT             | BRANCH     |
+-------+-------------------+------------+
| 16015 | Patricia McMilian | Arizona    |
| 17050 | Brent Ringer      | Illinois   |
| 17088 | Judy Wilson       | Arizona    |
| 18064 | Alex Mosley       | Illinois   |
+-------+-------------------+------------+
4 rows in set (1.88 sec)
```

The LIKE Operator

The LIKE Operator is another comparison keyword that can help enhance queries. You can use it to find all records with column values that satisfy a given pattern. It is also useful when you have no idea of the values stored in a table. A wild character '%' is used in such case.

For instance, assuming you want to find out the sales figures for agents whose name begins with 'B', you will write your query like this:

```
SELECT AGENT, SALES
FROM EMPLOYEE_SALES
WHERE AGENT LIKE 'B%';
```

The database returned two rows of agents whose names begin with 'B':

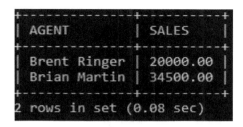

Besides the % wildcard character, you can also use the underscore symbol '_'. An underscore represents one character in search strings.

A similar query with the wildcard underscore character would be like:

SELECT AGENT, SALES
FROM EMPLOYEE_SALES
WHERE AGENT LIKE '_B';

Assuming you want to display the names of all agents with the letter 'a' as the second character, your query would be like:

SELECT AGENT FROM EMPLOYEE_SALES

WHERE AGENT LIKE '_a%';

The database returned four rows that match the condition:

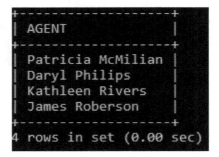

The BETWEEN Operator

The BETWEEN Operator is used with the AND logical operator to compare data within a specified range of values.

For instance, if you want to display the name and sales figure of agents whose sales are between 20,000 and 30,000, the query would look like this:

SELECT AGENT, SALES

FROM EMPLOYEE_SALES

WHERE SALES BETWEEN 20000.00 AND 30000.00;

The database returned 8 rows of data that match the specified range:

```
+--------------------+----------+
| AGENT              | SALES    |
+--------------------+----------+
| Lola Bowker        | 25000.00 |
| Brent Ringer       | 20000.00 |
| Daryl Philips      | 30000.00 |
| Kathleen Rivers    | 21000.00 |
| Alex Mosley        | 24500.00 |
| Russel Harris      | 26458.00 |
| James Roberson     | 29874.00 |
| Michael Bourne     | 22200.00 |
+--------------------+----------+
8 rows in set (0.06 sec)
```

The EXISTS Operator

The EXISTS clause is used in a subquery to find out if the subquery will return any row. When it returns at least a row, it indicates that the result satisfies the condition specified by the EXISTS clause and this will trigger the execution of the outer query.

To show how the EXISTS operator works, you can use the CUSTOMERS table and SALES table form the steel company as shown below:

CUSTOMERS		
CUST_CODE	CUSTOMER	ADDRESS
19238	AGC MERCHANDISE	3702 MY DRIVE WHITESTONE NY
18263	SHELL SUPPLIES	196 DALE AVENUE HANKAMER TX
19184	KENDRA PARKS	5349 FINCHAM ROAD SAN DIEGO CA
19435	XYZ BUSINESS	3205 MARSHVILLE ROAD POUGHKEEPSKIE NY
17432	CYCLING ACTS	2330 KINNEY STREET SPRINGFIELD MA
19253	POOLS AND PATIO	2371 HANIFAN LANE ROSWELL GA
18266	SINCERE DAYCARE	248 GREEN STREET SMITHVILLE TN
19123	BEST MAN STORE	3723 MIDDLEVILLE ROAD LOS ANGELES CA
18024	SPIN AND TURN	1242 SPRING STREET ELVASTON

		IL
19111	TOPSY TURVY CORP	362 ROSE AVENUE NEW ORLEANS LA

SALES				
INVOICE	PROD_ID	QUANTITY	SALES	CUST_CODE
114	1020	24	444.00	17432
115	1010	12	180.00	19123
116	1020	43	795.50	18024
117	1010	13	195.00	19111
118	1010	25	375.00	19238
119	1020	34	629.00	19253
120	1020	48	888.00	18024

The SALES table stores the sales transactions of the company. It contains five columns including the CUST_CODE column for each client who buys from the company.

The CUSTOMER table stores the CUST_CODE as well as the name and address of the customer. It does not provide data about particular transactions.

Let us say you want to view the names of the customer who purchased at least once. You will execute a subquery that will return a row for each customer who bought at least once from the company. Then the outer query will return the names of the customers that were identified as buyers in the SALES table.

Your statement would be like:

```
SELECT CUSTOMER  FROM CUSTOMERS
 WHERE 0 <>
  (SELECT COUNT(*)  FROM SALES
  WHERE SALES.CUST_CODE = CUSTOMERS.CUST_CODE);
```

When you execute the query, the database will return six rows of results:

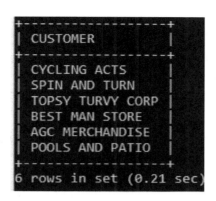

```
+-------------------+
| CUSTOMER          |
+-------------------+
| CYCLING ACTS      |
| SPIN AND TURN     |
| TOPSY TURVY CORP  |
| BEST MAN STORE    |
| AGC MERCHANDISE   |
| POOLS AND PATIO   |
+-------------------+
6 rows in set (0.21 sec)
```

While there are seven records in the SALES table, one customer purchased twice so only six customers were returned.

The DISTINCT Operator

The DISTINCT operator is used with the SELECT command to search for unique values in a specified column.

Columns frequently contain duplicate value and if you need to display data, which are unique, you can use the SELECT DISTINCT clause on one or more tables.

Here is the syntax:

```
SELECT DISTINCT column1, column2, ...
FROM table_name;
```

The SALES table below has duplicate records in some columns:

```
+----------+----------+----------+----------+-----------+
| INVOICE  | PROD_ID  | QUANTITY | SALES    | CUST_CODE |
+----------+----------+----------+----------+-----------+
|      114 |     1020 |       24 | 444.00   |     17432 |
|      115 |     1010 |       12 | 180.00   |     19123 |
|      116 |     1020 |       43 | 795.50   |     18024 |
|      117 |     1010 |       13 | 195.00   |     19111 |
|      118 |     1010 |       25 | 375.00   |     19238 |
|      119 |     1020 |       34 | 629.00   |     19253 |
|      120 |     1020 |       48 | 888.00   |     18024 |
+----------+----------+----------+----------+-----------+
7 rows in set (4.88 sec)
```

If you want to display only the unique CUST_CODE data, you can execute this statement:

SELECT DISTINCT CUST_CODE
FROM SALES;

Here is the output:

```
+-----------+
| CUST_CODE |
+-----------+
|     17432 |
|     19123 |
|     18024 |
|     19111 |
|     19238 |
|     19253 |
+-----------+
```

The ANY Operator

The ANY operator is used to compare a value to every query result or list items. It returns true if the inner query returns at least a single row. This logical operator must be placed after a comparison operator.

The following example uses the CUSTOMERS table and SALES table of steelcompany database. The ANY operator is used to display the name and address of the customer who purchased a product from the company as reported in Invoice 118:

SELECT CUSTOMER, ADDRESS FROM CUSTOMERS
WHERE CUST_CODE = ANY(
SELECT CUST_CODE FROM SALES

WHERE INVOICE=118);

The query returned a row of data, which matched the condition:

```
+-----------------+------------------------------------+
| CUSTOMER        | ADDRESS                            |
+-----------------+------------------------------------+
| AGC MERCHANDISE | 3702 MY DRIVE WHITESTONE NY        |
+-----------------+------------------------------------+
1 row in set (1.83 sec)
```

LIKE and Wildcards

The LIKE operator is used with wildcards to perform pattern comparison in queries. You can use it within the WHERE clause of an UPDATE, DELETE, INSERT, or SELECT statement.

You can use the LIKE operator with two wildcard symbols:

percent sign: %
The % wildcard symbol represents one, zero, or multiple characters.

underscore: _

The underscore _ symbol represents a character or number.

You can use the percent and underscore operators in one clause. In addition, you can specify more than one condition using the AND or OR operators.

The following statements are examples of the usage of the LIKE operator with wildcard symbols:

WHERE Name LIKE '%we%'
Finds values with "we" in any position

WHERE Last_Name LIKE 'C%
Finds values that begin with "C"

WHERE Supp_Name LIKE '_r%'
Finds values with "o" in the second position

WHERE Stud_Name LIKE 'H_%_%'
Finds values that begin with 'H' and have at least 3 characters

WHERE Emp_Name LIKE 'C%n'

Finds values that begin with "C" and ends with "n"

WHERE SALARY LIKE '4000%'
Searches for values that begin at 4000.

WHERE SALARY LIKE '%7800%'
Searches for values with 7800 in any position.

WHERE ALLOWANCE LIKE '_50%'
Searches for values with 50 in the second and third positions

WHERE SALES LIKE '2_%_%'
Finds values that start with 2 with a length of at least 3 characters

WHERE POSITION LIKE 'S%'
Finds values that begin with "S"

WHERE Cust_Name LIKE '%s'
Finds values that end with "s"

WHERE Agent_Name LIKE '%er%'

Searches for values that have "er" in any position

WHERE Cust_Name LIKE '_s%'

Finds values that have "s" in the second position

WHERE Emp_Name LIKE 'H_%_%'

Finds values that start with "H" with a minimum length of 3 characters

WHERE Employee_Name LIKE 'M%e'

Finds values that begin with "M" and ends with "E"

When using the data type char for pattern matching, bear in mind that the char type is padded at the end to fill the specified field length. Using the LIKE keyword to match patterns at the end of a string could produce unexpected results if you don't consider the padding at the end of the char type data.

NULL Value

In SQL, the word NULL represents a missing value. When a field has a NULL value, it means that it has no value. A field with a NULL value is not the same as a field with zero value or one that contains spaces.

When a field is optional or was not declared with the NOT NULL constraint, you may or may not add a value to it when you're inserting or updating a record. By default, SQL saves the field with a NULL value.

Testing for NULL Values

The operators IS NULL and IS NOT NULL are used to test for NULL values in a table.

Syntax:

IS NULL

```
SELECT column_names
FROM table_name
WHERE column_name IS NULL;
```

IS NOT NULL

```
SELECT column_names
FROM table_name
WHERE column_name IS NOT NULL;
```

Chapter 13: SQL Functions

An SQL function is a sub-program that you can use repeatedly in database applications to process and manipulate data. MySQL, Oracle, Microsoft SQL, and other major SQL versions offer a great range of built-in functions that can be used to automate routine work in SQL and perform a myriad of tasks. SQL implementations also enable users to create their own functions.

SQL Functions can be classified as either built-in or user-defined.

SQL's standard or built-in functions are pre-defined SQL database formula that users can call for calculations or data processing. On the other hand, user-defined functions are those which are defined by users to perform a particular task.

Using functions can be advantageous in most cases. Here are the most common reasons why you should use them:

- Functions are reusable code that can save considerable programming time and effort.

- Functions break down complex programming logic into smaller, simpler, and more manageable parts.

- Functions can help enhance the efficiency and performance of databases.

Built-in Functions

SQL's built-in functions are grouped into two main types: aggregate and scalar.

Aggregate Functions

Aggregate functions operate on a set of database fields and produce a single value. The output can be numerical or string values.

SQL supports the following aggregate functions:

COUNT()
AVG()
SUM()
MAX()

MIN()

The COUNT() function

The COUNT() function returns the number of rows that match the given conditions.

Syntax:


```
SELECT COUNT (<expression>)
FROM table_name;
```


The expression in the above statement can refer to a column name or an arithmetic operation. In addition, you can specify (*) to indicate that you want to calculate the total records in the table.

For examples in the usage of aggregate functions, you will be using the EMPLOYEES table of the steelcompany database:

EMP_NO	FNAME	LNAME	DEPARTMENT	SALARY
000011	Janice	Winkle	Sales	5000.00
000012	Alan	Mars	Sales	3000.00
000013	Michelle	Pars	Finance	4000.00
000014	Andrew	Winters	Finance	5000.00
000015	Erma	Gherd	HR	5000.00
000016	Julius	Hanes	Sales	2000.00
000017	Arnold	Givens	HR	4000.00
000018	Anthony	Wilson	Sales	3000.00
000019	Megan	Jung	Finance	3000.00
000020	Shane	Paulsen	Sales	3500.00

Using the COUNT function, you can perform a simple operation such as calculating the number of rows that are stored in the EMPLOYEES table. You can use this statement for that purpose:

```
SELECT COUNT(EMP_NO)
FROM EMPLOYEES;
```

The function returned 10 records:

```
+----------------+
| COUNT(EMP_NO)  |
+----------------+
|            10  |
+----------------+
1 row in set (0.64 sec)
```

You may also omit the column name and use the * as the parameter for the COUNT function:

SELECT COUNT(*)
FROM EMPLOYEES;

The above statement will return the same result. Take note, however, that the two statements produced the same results only because the column EMP_NO does not contain a NULL value. Assuming the EMP_NO columns has a NULL value, it will not be included in the COUNT(EMP_NO) operation as a result but it will be included in the COUNT(*) operation.

You can use COUNT() function with the GROUP by clause to count the occurrence of records that match the grouping criteria.

For example, you can calculate the number of employees for each department using this statement:

SELECT DEPARTMENT, COUNT(*) FROM EMPLOYEES GROUP BY DEPARTMENT;

Here is the result:

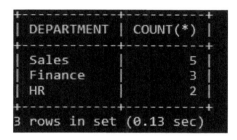

You can also use the COUNT() function with DISTINCT to calculate the number of distinct entries. For example, you may want to find out how many distinct departments are stored in the EMPLOYEES table. You will use the following statement for that purpose:

SELECT COUNT (DISTINCT DEPARTMENT)

FROM EMPLOYEES;

The database returned 3 distinct departments from the EMPLOYEES table:

```
+----------------------------------+
| COUNT(DISTINCT DEPARTMENT)       |
+----------------------------------+
|                               3  |
+----------------------------------+
1 row in set (0.05 sec)
```

You can also use the COUNT() function with the WHERE clause to select table values that match the condition.

For example, to determine the number of rows where the salary is more than 4,000.00, you can execute this statement:

SELECT COUNT(*) as "More than 4000.00"
FROM EMPLOYEES
WHERE SALARY >4000.00;

The database returned 3:

```
+---------------------+
| More than 4,000.00  |
+---------------------+
|                  3  |
+---------------------+
1 row in set (0.00 sec)
```

The AVG Function()

The AVG() function is used to calculate the average value of columns with numeric data type. It operates on the non-NULL values and returns their average.

Here is the basic syntax:

AVG ([ALL | DISTINCT] expression)

To use the AVG() function in a SELECT statement, you will use this syntax:

```
SELECT AVG (<expression>)
FROM "table_name";
```

The expression can refer to a column name or an arithmetic operation. Arithmetic operations can have single or multiple columns.

The first example in this section will use the EMPLOYEES table in the steelcompany database:

```
+--------+----------+----------+------------+----------+
| EMP_NO | FNAME    | LNAME    | DEPARTMENT | SALARY   |
+--------+----------+----------+------------+----------+
| 11     | Janice   | Winkle   | Sales      | 5000.00  |
| 12     | Alan     | Mars     | Sales      | 3000.00  |
| 13     | Michelle | Pars     | Finance    | 4000.00  |
| 14     | Andrew   | Winters  | Finance    | 5000.00  |
| 15     | Erma     | Gherd    | HR         | 5000.00  |
| 16     | Julius   | Hanes    | Sales      | 2000.00  |
| 17     | Arnold   | Givens   | HR         | 4000.00  |
| 18     | Anthony  | Wilson   | Sales      | 3000.00  |
| 19     | Megan    | Jung     | Finance    | 3000.00  |
| 20     | Shane    | Paulsen  | Sales      | 3500.00  |
+--------+----------+----------+------------+----------+
```

To demonstrate, if you want to determine the average salary of the employees, you can use the SELECT statement with the AVG() function:

SELECT AVG(SALARY) FROM EMPLOYEES;

Here is the output:

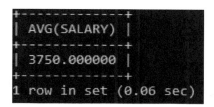

The database returned the amount 3750.00 as the average salary. You can check this by dividing the total salary by the number of employees.

You can also extract the average of all distinct values using the DISTINCT operator.

SELECT AVG(DISTINCT SALARY) AS "AVERAGE DISTINCT SALARY"
FROM EMPLOYEES;

Take note that since the statement aliased the average distinct salary as "AVERAGE DISTINCT SALARY", the result will be returned with that caption.

Here is the output:

```
+--------------------------+
| AVERAGE DISTINCT SALARY  |
+--------------------------+
|              3500.000000 |
+--------------------------+
1 row in set (0.36 sec)
```

In some instances, you may need to qualify the result by using the AVG() function with the GROUP BY keyword.

In the above example, you can invoke the AVG() function to output a specific department name and the average salary of that department.

To demonstrate, you can use the AVG() function to return the average salary of the Sales department with this statement:

```
SELECT DEPARTMENT, AVG(SALARY) AS "Average Salary"
FROM EMPLOYEES
WHERE DEPARTMENT = 'Sales'
GROUP BY DEPARTMENT;
```

Here is the output:

You can check this manually by adding the salary of all employees in the Sales Department and dividing the result by the total number of employees in the Sales Department:

5,000.00 + 3,000.00 + 2,000.00 + 3,000.00 + 3,500.00
        16,500.00

Divided by the Number of Employees in Sales Department
        5

Average Salary (Sales Department)
3,300.00

Mathematical Expression Within the AVG() Function

So far, we have only used single expression as a parameter of the AVG() function. The AVG() function is not limited to single expressions. You may also pass a formula or mathematical operation.

To demonstrate, you will use the ANNUAL_REPORT table of the abccompany database:

```
+---------------+----------+--------------+--------------+
| PRODUCT_ID    | VOLUME   | TOTAL_COST   | TOTAL_SALES  |
+---------------+----------+--------------+--------------+
|          1010 |    34500 |     86250.00 |    103500.00 |
|          1020 |    12066 |     28958.40 |     37645.92 |
|          2010 |    67234 |    161361.60 |    201702.00 |
|          2020 |    11066 |     25451.80 |     31814.75 |
|          3010 |    23098 |     53125.40 |     64812.99 |
|          3030 |    22472 |     47191.20 |     60404.74 |
|          4010 |     9876 |     20739.60 |     37331.28 |
|          4020 |     1254 |      2658.48 |      4253.57 |
|          5010 |    46987 |     84576.60 |    105720.75 |
|          5020 |    24926 |     55086.46 |     70510.67 |
+---------------+----------+--------------+--------------+
```

Assuming you want to calculate the average profit (TOTAL_SALES less TOTAL_COST), you can use the following statement:

SELECT AVG(TOTAL_SALES – TOTAL_COST) AS "Average Profit"

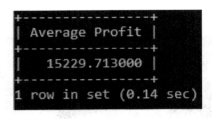

```
+-----------------+
| Average Profit  |
+-----------------+
|    15229.713000 |
+-----------------+
1 row in set (0.14 sec)
```

If you will compute the average manually, this is how you will do it:

Total Sales	717,696.66
Total Cost	565,399.54
Total Profit	152,297.12
Divided by number of products	10
Average Profit	15,229.71

You can also perform mathematical operations inside the AVG() function. If you were to compute for the average commission of 15% on sales, you can use this statement:

SELECT AVG(TOTAL_SALES * .15) AS "Average Commission" FROM ANNUAL_REPORT;

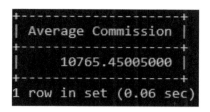

If you were to compute it manually, here is how you would have calculated the result:

Total Sales	717,696.66
Divided by number of products	10.00
Average Sales	71,769.67
Multiplied by Commission Rate	15%
Average Commission	10,765.45

The SUM() Function

The SQL SUM() function is an aggregate function that you can use to return the total for all selected columns or expression.

Syntax:

SUM ([ALL | DISTINCT] expression)

The expression parameter can be an arithmetic operation or a column name. Arithmetic operations may involve one or multiple columns.

For examples in this section, we will be using the COST table. The COST table is stored in the abccompany database and has the following data:

PRODUCT_ID	VOLUME	TLABOR	TMATERIALS
1010	34,500	51,750.00	34,500.00
1020	12,066	14,479.20	14,479.20
2010	67,234	48,408.48	112,953.12
2020	11,066	15,271.08	10,180.72
3010	23,098	26,562.70	26,562.70
3030	22,472	18,876.48	28,314.72
4010	9,876	8,295.84	12,443.76
4020	1,254	1,595.09	1,063.39
5010	46,987	59,203.62	25,372.98
5020	24,926	33,051.88	22,034.58

The most basic SUM() operation you can perform with the COST table is adding the values of a single column.

For example, if you want to add the values in the TLABOR column, your statement could be:

SELECT SUM(TLABOR)
FROM COST;

Output:

```
+--------------+
| SUM(TLABOR)  |
+--------------+
|    287905.17 |
+--------------+
1 row in set (0.01 sec)
```

To get the total of the TMATERIALS column:

SELECT SUM(TMATERIALS) AS "Total Materials":
FROM COST;

Output:

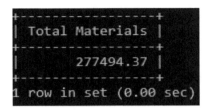

```
+-------------------+
| Total Materials   |
+-------------------+
|         277494.37 |
+-------------------+
1 row in set (0.00 sec)
```

You can also use the SUM() function to add the total of the TMATERIALS AND TLABOR columns.

Here is the statement:

SELECT SUM (TMATERIALS + TLABOR)
FROM COST;

Output:

```
+---------------------------+
| SUM(TMATERIALS + TLABOR)  |
+---------------------------+
|                565399.54  |
+---------------------------+
1 row in set (0.00 sec)
```

You can countercheck the result by adding 287,905.17 and 277494.37, the sum of the TLABOR and TMATERIALS column.

Getting the Sum of Values from a Specific Row

You may want to calculate the total labor and materials for a specific product. For this purpose, you will use SUM with the WHERE clause to select the records that match the given condition.

For example, if you want to calculate and view the sum of TMATERIALS and TLABOR for PRODUCT_ID 3010, you can execute this statement:

```
SELECT SUM (TLABOR AND TMATERIALS)
FROM COST
WHERE PRODUCT_ID = '3010';
```

Output:

```
+-----------------------------+
| SUM(TLABOR + TMATERIALS)    |
+-----------------------------+
|                   53125.40  |
+-----------------------------+
1 row in set (0.00 sec)
```

Since there is only one record that meets the condition, the database returned the total of the values in the TMATERIALS and TLABOR of PRDUCT_ID 3010.

For the next example, we will be using the SALES table stored in the steelcompany database:

INVOICE	PROD_ID	QUANTITY	SALES	CUST_CODE
114	1020	24	444.00	17432
115	1010	12	180.00	19123
116	1020	43	795.50	18024
117	1010	13	195.00	19111
118	1010	25	375.00	19238
119	1020	34	629.00	19253
120	1020	48	888.00	18024

The SALES table shows the partial sales records of the Steel Company. If you want to display the total sales for product 1020, you can use this statement:

SELECT SUM (SALES)
FROM SALES
WHERE PROD_ID = 1020;

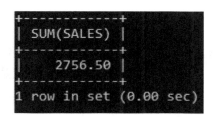

The database returned the total of 2756.50. You can countercheck the result manually by adding the sales figures for PROD_ID 1020: 444.00 + 795.50 + 629.00 + 888.00.

The next example will show how you can use the SQL SUM()
with the SQL() COUNT together to return the total sales for all
products in the SALES table and the number of records for each
product.

You can use the SELECT statement below to display the total
sales for the products (Product ID 1010 and 1020) and the
record count for each PROD_ID stored in the SALES table:

SELECT PROD_ID, SUM(SALES),
COUNT(PROD_ID)
FROM SALES
GROUP BY PROD_ID;

Here is the result:

```
+---------+-----------+----------------+
| PROD_ID | SUM(SALES) | COUNT(PROD_ID) |
+---------+-----------+----------------+
|    1020 |   2756.50 |              4 |
|    1010 |    750.00 |              3 |
+---------+-----------+----------------+
2 rows in set (0.11 sec)
```

The MAX Function

The MAX() function is an aggregate function that can be used to obtain the largest or maximum value of an expression or column. You will find this function useful when you want to determine the highest among the selected column values.

Syntax:

SELECT MAX (<expression>)
FROM table_name;

Take note that the parameter of a MAX() function could be an arithmetic operation or a column name. In addition, arithmetic operations can have multiple columns.

To demonstrate the usage of the MAX() function, we will be using the COST table from the abccompany database with the following data:

```
+---------------+----------+-------------+------------+
| PRODUCT_ID    | VOLUME   | TMATERIALS  | TLABOR     |
+---------------+----------+-------------+------------+
|          1010 |    34500 |    51750.00 |   34500.00 |
|          1020 |    12066 |    14479.20 |   14479.20 |
|          2010 |    67234 |    48408.48 |  112953.12 |
|          2020 |    11066 |    15271.08 |   10180.72 |
|          3010 |    23098 |    26562.70 |   26562.70 |
|          3030 |    22472 |    18876.48 |   28314.72 |
|          4010 |     9876 |     8295.84 |   12443.76 |
|          4020 |     1254 |     1595.09 |    1063.39 |
|          5010 |    46987 |    59203.62 |   25372.98 |
|          5020 |    24926 |    33051.88 |   22034.58 |
+---------------+----------+-------------+------------+
10 rows in set (0.16 sec)
```

Let us say you want to display the product with the highest volume, you can use the following statement:

SELECT MAX (VOLUME)
FROM COST;

Output:

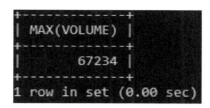

```
+--------------+
| MAX(VOLUME)  |
+--------------+
|        67234 |
+--------------+
1 row in set (0.00 sec)
```

The database returned Product ID 1010 with a volume of 67,234 as the highest value.

You may want to calculate the highest value among the total costs of each product. For this, you will use an arithmetic operation to add the total labor and total materials (TLABOR + TMATERIALS) columns.

You will use this statement:

SELECT MAX(TMATERIALS + TLABOR)
FROM COST;

Output:

```
+---------------------------+
| MAX(TMATERIALS + TLABOR)  |
+---------------------------+
|                 161361.60 |
+---------------------------+
1 row in set (0.00 sec)
```

The query returned Product ID 1010 with total cost of 161,361.60 as result.

MAX() Function with GROUP BY Clause

The SELECT STATEMENT can take one or more columns besides the column passed as parameter in the MAX() function. In such cases, these columns should be specified in a GROUP BY clause.

You will use this syntax for that operation:

SELECT column1, column2, column3... , MAX (<expression>)
FROM table_name
GROUP BY column1, column2, column3...,;

To demonstrate, we will be using the SALES table stored in the steelcompany database with the following data:

```
+----------+----------+----------+----------+-----------+
| INVOICE  | PROD_ID  | QUANTITY | SALES    | CUST_CODE |
+----------+----------+----------+----------+-----------+
|      114 |     1020 |       24 | 444.00   |     17432 |
|      115 |     1010 |       12 | 180.00   |     19123 |
|      116 |     1020 |       43 | 795.50   |     18024 |
|      117 |     1010 |       13 | 195.00   |     19111 |
|      118 |     1010 |       25 | 375.00   |     19238 |
|      119 |     1020 |       34 | 629.00   |     19253 |
|      120 |     1020 |       48 | 888.00   |     18024 |
+----------+----------+----------+----------+-----------+
7 rows in set (0.07 sec)
```

Assuming you want to display the Product ID and the highest
sales value for each product, you will have to use the GROUP BY
clause with the MAX() function in the SELECT statement.

Here is the statement:

SELECT PROD_ID, MAX(SALES)
FROM SALES
GROUP BY PROD_ID;

Output:

```
+----------+-------------+
| PROD_ID  | MAX(SALES)  |
+----------+-------------+
|    1020  |     888.00  |
|    1010  |     375.00  |
+----------+-------------+
2 rows in set (0.03 sec)
```

The query returned two rows showing the highest sales value for
each product code in the SALES table.

You may want to view the above data in a specific order. You can
use the ORDER by CLAUSE with the GROUP BY clause and the
MAX() function using this statement:

SELECT PROD_ID, MAX(SALES)
FROM SALES
GROUP BY PROD_ID
ORDER BY PROD_ID;

Output:

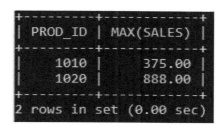

By default, the query returned the data in ascending order based on product id.

SQL Max() with GROUP BY and HAVING Clause

In the preceding example, the query returned the highest sales value for each product. You can modify the query result further by using the HAVING clause with the GROUP BY clause and MAX() in the SELECT statement.

For example, if you want to display the highest value per product only if it is more than 500.00, you can use this statement:

SELECT PROD_ID, MAX(SALES)
FROM SALES

GROUP BY PROD_ID

HAVING MAX(SALES) >500.00;

Output:

```
+-----------+---------------+
| PROD_ID | MAX(SALES) |
+-----------+---------------+
|    1020 |        888.00 |
+-----------+---------------+
1 row in set (0.03 sec)
```

Only one product satisfied the condition and the modified query returned only one row for Product ID 1020 with sales amount of 888.00.

The MIN() Function

The MIN() function is an aggregate function that can be used to obtain the lowest or minimum value of an expression or column. You will also find this function useful when you want to determine the lowest among the selected column values.

Syntax:

SELECT MIN (<expression>)
FROM table_name;

The parameters of a MIN() function could be an arithmetic operation or a column name. In addition, arithmetic operations can have multiple columns.

To demonstrate the usage of the MIN() function, we will be using the COST table from the abccompany database with the following data:

```
+---------------+---------+-----------+-----------+
| PRODUCT_ID    | VOLUME  | TMATERIALS | TLABOR    |
+---------------+---------+-----------+-----------+
|          1010 |   34500 |  51750.00 |  34500.00 |
|          1020 |   12066 |  14479.20 |  14479.20 |
|          2010 |   67234 |  48408.48 | 112953.12 |
|          2020 |   11066 |  15271.08 |  10180.72 |
|          3010 |   23098 |  26562.70 |  26562.70 |
|          3030 |   22472 |  18876.48 |  28314.72 |
|          4010 |    9876 |   8295.84 |  12443.76 |
|          4020 |    1254 |   1595.09 |   1063.39 |
|          5010 |   46987 |  59203.62 |  25372.98 |
|          5020 |   24926 |  33051.88 |  22034.58 |
+---------------+---------+-----------+-----------+
10 rows in set (0.16 sec)
```

If you want to display the product with the highest volume, you can use the MIN() function in a SELECT statement as shown below:

SELECT MIN (VOLUME)
FROM COST;

Output:

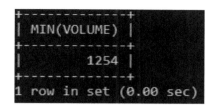

The query returned 1,254 as the lowest value in the VOLUME column.

You may also want to find the highest value among the total costs of each product. You will have to use an arithmetic operation to add the total labor and materials columns (TMATERIALS + TLABOR).

Here is the statement:

SELECT MIN(TMATERIALS + TLABOR)
FROM COST;

Output:

```
+---------------------------+
| MIN(TMATERIALS + TLABOR)  |
+---------------------------+
|                  2658.48  |
+---------------------------+
1 row in set (0.02 sec)
```

The query returned 2,658.48 as the lowest total cost among the products in the COST table.

MIN() Function with GROUP BY Clause

The SELECT STATEMENT can take one or more columns besides the column passed as parameter in the MIN() function. These columns should be specified in a GROUP BY clause.

Here is the syntax:

SELECT column1, column2, column3... , MIN (<expression>)
FROM table_name
GROUP BY column1, column2, column3...,;

To demonstrate, we will be using the SALES table stored in the steelcompany database with the following data:

```
+---------+---------+----------+---------+-----------+
| INVOICE | PROD_ID | QUANTITY | SALES   | CUST_CODE |
+---------+---------+----------+---------+-----------+
|     114 |    1020 |       24 |  444.00 |     17432 |
|     115 |    1010 |       12 |  180.00 |     19123 |
|     116 |    1020 |       43 |  795.50 |     18024 |
|     117 |    1010 |       13 |  195.00 |     19111 |
|     118 |    1010 |       25 |  375.00 |     19238 |
|     119 |    1020 |       34 |  629.00 |     19253 |
|     120 |    1020 |       48 |  888.00 |     18024 |
+---------+---------+----------+---------+-----------+
7 rows in set (0.00 sec)
```

If you want to display the Product ID and the lowest sales for each product, you will need to use the GROUP BY clause with the MAX() function in the SELECT statement.

Here's the statement:

SELECT PROD_ID, MIN(SALES)
FROM SALES
GROUP BY PROD_ID;

Output:

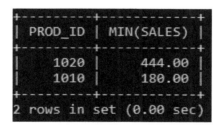

The query returned two rows showing the lowest sales value for each product code in the SALES table.

You may prefer to view the above result in a particular order. For that purpose, you can use the ORDER BY CLAUSE with the GROUP BY clause and the MAX() function in the SELECT statement.

For example:

SELECT PROD_ID, MIN(SALES)
FROM SALES
GROUP BY PROD_ID
ORDER BY PROD_ID;

Output:

```
+------------+--------------+
|  PROD_ID   | MIN(SALES)   |
+------------+--------------+
|      1010  |      180.00  |
|      1020  |      444.00  |
+------------+--------------+
2 rows in set (0.02 sec)
```

The query returned the data in ascending order based on product id. This is the default order.

SQL Max() with GROUP BY and HAVING Clause

In the above example, the query returned the highest sales value for each product. You can qualify the query result further by using the HAVING clause with the GROUP BY clause and MAX() in the SELECT statement.

For instance, if you want to display the lowest value per product only if it is less than 300.00, you can run this statement:

SELECT PROD_ID, MIN(SALES)

FROM SALES

GROUP BY PROD_ID

HAVING MIN(SALES) < 300.00;

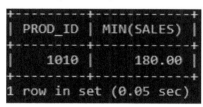

Only one product satisfied the condition and the modified query returned only one row for Product ID 1010 with sales amount of 180.00.

Scalar Functions

Scalar functions work on data or user input individually and returns a single value. SQL supports several scalar functions.

The following are the most frequently used scalar functions in SQL:

ROUND()
UCASE()
LCASE()
LEN()
MID()
NOW()
TRANSLATE()
TRIM()
FORMAT()

The ROUND Function

The ROUND() function is used to round a number to a specified precision or decimal places. It returns a number rounded to the closest integer. If you supply another argument for the decimal place, it returns the given number rounded to that precision.

Syntax:

ROUND (expression, [decimal place])

The expression refers to the number to be rounded off while the decimal place specifies the decimal place that will be returned. If you do not provide a second argument, the given number will be rounded off to the nearest tens.

To see how the ROUND() function works, you can try this statement:

SELECT ROUND(100.76531);

Output:

```
+-----------------+
| ROUND(100.76531) |
+-----------------+
|              101 |
+-----------------+
1 row in set (0.03 sec)
```

Since no argument was provided, the number was rounded off to the nearest tens.

Next, you can try the ROUND() function with a decimal place argument:

SELECT ROUND(100.76531, 2);

Output:

```
+--------------------+
| ROUND(100.76531,2) |
+--------------------+
|             100.77 |
+--------------------+
1 row in set (0.00 sec)
```

The number was rounded off to two decimal places as specified.

The decimal place argument should be positive if you want a proper round off operation on decimals. Providing a negative decimal place argument will remove all decimal places.

Example:

```
+---------------------+
| ROUND(100.76531,-2) |
+---------------------+
|                 100 |
+---------------------+
1 row in set (0.00 sec)
```

The above ROUND() operation returned an integer rounded off to the nearest ones and dropped all decimal numbers.

In the following example, you will be working with the CLASS_GRADES table in the TOPNOTCHSCHOOL database:

ID	FNAME	LNAME	GRADE
1	Tom	Crane	95.7654
2	Jack	Poulerd	96.3421
3	Randy	Young	95.4378
4	Alicia	Stone	97.5432
5	Jamie	Berger	99.5643
6	Millicent	Green	98.4359
7	Shane	Duff	97.6286
8	Roberta	Croft	94.9574
9	Jack	Hart	93.1289
10	Charlie	Rich	94.2174

```
+----+-----------+----------+--------+
| ID | FNAME     | LNAME    | GRADE  |
+----+-----------+----------+--------+
|  1 | Tom       | Crane    | 95.77  |
|  2 | Jack      | Poulerd  | 96.34  |
|  3 | Randy     | Young    | 95.44  |
|  4 | Alicia    | Stone    | 97.54  |
|  5 | Jamie     | Berger   | 99.56  |
|  6 | Millicent | Green    | 98.44  |
|  7 | Shane     | Duff     | 97.63  |
|  8 | Roberta   | Croft    | 94.96  |
|  9 | Jack      | Hart     | 93.13  |
| 10 | Charlie   | Rich     | 94.22  |
+----+-----------+----------+--------+
```

If you want to round off the students' grades to the nearest tenths, you will have to provide the GRADE as the main argument and supply 1 as the second argument for the decimal place.

Here's the statement:

SELECT FNAME, LNAME, ROUND (GRADE, 1) AS "Rounded Grade"
FROM CLASS_GRADE

Output:

```
+------------+------------+----------------+
| FNAME      | LNAME      | Rounded Grade  |
+------------+------------+----------------+
| Tom        | Crane      |           95.8 |
| Jack       | Poulerd    |           96.3 |
| Randy      | Young      |           95.4 |
| Alicia     | Stone      |           97.5 |
| Jamie      | Berger     |           99.6 |
| Millicent  | Green      |           98.4 |
| Shane      | Duff       |           97.6 |
| Roberta    | Croft      |           95.0 |
| Jack       | Hart       |           93.1 |
| Charlie    | Rich       |           94.2 |
+------------+------------+----------------+
```

The query with the ROUND() function returned the grades rounded off to the nearest tenths.

If you want to round the grades to the nearest tens, you will have to provide a negative second argument for the ROUND() function.

Example:
SELECT   FNAME,   LNAME,   ROUND   (Grade,   -1)   AS Rounded_Grade
FROM CLASS_GRADES;

Output:

```
+-----------+-----------+-----------------+
| FNAME     | LNAME     | Rounded Grade   |
+-----------+-----------+-----------------+
| Tom       | Crane     |             100 |
| Jack      | Poulerd   |             100 |
| Randy     | Young     |             100 |
| Alicia    | Stone     |             100 |
| Jamie     | Berger    |             100 |
| Millicent | Green     |             100 |
| Shane     | Duff      |             100 |
| Roberta   | Croft     |              90 |
| Jack      | Hart      |              90 |
| Charlie   | Rich      |              90 |
+-----------+-----------+-----------------+
10 rows in set (0.00 sec)
```

The query returned the grades without the decimal places and rounded the grades to the nearest tens.

UCASE()

The UCASE function is used to convert a field's value to uppercase.

Syntax:

SELECT UCASE(column_name) FROM table_name;

253

For example, to display the values in uppercase of the LASTNAME column of the EMPLOYEES table shown below, you will use this statement:

SELECT UCASE(LASTNAME) FROM EMPLOYEES;

```
+---------+-----------+----------+-----------+----------------+-----------+
| ID      | FIRSTNAME | LASTNAME | JOBTITLE  | DEPARTMENT     | MONTHLYPAY|
+---------+-----------+----------+-----------+----------------+-----------+
| 190005  | John      | Watson   | Dispatcher| Administration |  5000.00  |
| 190006  | Mickey    | Malone   | Officer   | Operations     |  7000.00  |
| 190007  | Kirsten   | Dunk     | Manager   | Administration |  8000.00  |
| 190008  | Chinkee   | Stuart   | Agent     | Sales          |  6000.00  |
| 190009  | Sherry    | Lynx     | Executive | Management     | 10000.00  |
+---------+-----------+----------+-----------+----------------+-----------+
```

Output:

```
+-------------------+
| UCASE(LASTNAME)   |
+-------------------+
| WATSON            |
| MALONE            |
| DUNK              |
| STUART            |
| LYNX              |
+-------------------+
```

LCASE()

This function is used to convert field values to lowercase.

Syntax:

SELECT LCASE(column_name) FROM table_name;

For example, to display the values of the LASTNAME column in the lowercase, you will use this statement:

SELECT LCASE(LASTNAME) FROM EMPLOYEES;

Output:

LEN()

The LEN() function is used to return the length of column values.

Syntax:

SELECT LENGTH(column_name) FROM table_name;

For example, to display the length of the values stored in the DEPARTMENT column, you will use this statement:

SELECT LENGTH(DEPARTMENT) FROM EMPLOYEES;

Output:

```
+--------------------+
| LENGTH(DEPARTMENT) |
+--------------------+
|                 14 |
|                 10 |
|                 14 |
|                  5 |
|                 10 |
+--------------------+
5 rows in set (0.00 sec)
```

MID()

The MID() function is used to extract text from text fields.

Syntax:

SELECT MID(column_name,start,length) AS some_name FROM table_name;

The start argument refers one, the first position.

For example, to display the first three characters of the JOBTITLE column of the EMPLOYEES table, you will use this statement:

SELECT MID(JOBTITLE, 1, 3) AS "First Three" FROM EMPLOYEES;

Output:

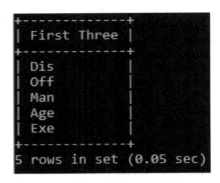

```
+--------------+
| First Three  |
+--------------+
| Dis          |
| Off          |
| Man          |
| Age          |
| Exe          |
+--------------+
5 rows in set (0.05 sec)
```

NOW()

This function is used to return the current system time and date.

Syntax:

SELECT NOW() FROM table_name;

For example, to display the First Name, Last Name and the current date and time from the EMPLOYEES table, you will use this statement:

SELECT FIRSTNAME, LASTNAME, NOW() AS "Date & Time" FROM EMPLOYEES;

Output:

```
+------------+------------+----------------------+
| FIRSTNAME  | LASTNAME   | Date & Time          |
+------------+------------+----------------------+
| John       | Watson     | 2019-09-03 06:34:57  |
| Mickey     | Malone     | 2019-09-03 06:34:57  |
| Kirsten    | Dunk       | 2019-09-03 06:34:57  |
| Chinkee    | Stuart     | 2019-09-03 06:34:57  |
| Sherry     | Lynx       | 2019-09-03 06:34:57  |
+------------+------------+----------------------+
5 rows in set (0.03 sec)
```

Summary

Functions are predefined database formula that can be called to perform data processing tasks or calculations. SQL provides built-in functions and the facilities to create user-defined functions. SQL supports aggregate and scalar built in functions.

Aggregate functions are those that work on a set of database fields and include the COUNT(), AVG(), SUM(), MAX(), and MIN() functions.

Scalar functions are built-in functions that work on individual inputs. They include functions such as Round(), UCASE(),

259

LCASE(), LEN(), MID(), NOW(), TRANSLATE(), TRIM(), and FORMAT().

Practice Exercises

Practice Exercise 13-1

For this exercise, you will use the ORDERS table with the following data:

ORDERNO	ORDERDATE	PRODUCTID	QUANTITY	PRICE
20100123	2019-09-01	101001	98	28.99
20100124	2019-09-05	101005	46	16.55
20100125	2019-09-07	101001	87	28.99
20100126	2019-09-10	101008	92	25.77
20100127	2019-09-11	101005	15	16.55
20100128	2019-09-12	101008	98	25.77
20100129	2019-09-13	101009	46	50.55
20100131	2019-09-20	101007	92	29.76
20100132	2019-09-21	101009	15	50.55
20100133	2019-09-22	101020	22	98.40

Write the statement that will count the number of records in the ORDERS table. Display the result as "No. of Records".

Practice Exercise 13-2

Write the statement that will return the average price of products from the ORDERS table. Display the results as "Average Price"

Practice Exercise 13-3

Write the statement that will add the Quantity ordered for PRODUCT ID No. 101005. Show the result as "Total Quantity On Order"

Solutions

Practice Exercise 13-1

SELECT COUNT(ORDERNO) AS "No. of Records"
FROM ORDERS;

Output:

Practice Exercise 13-2

SELECT AVG(PRICE) AS "Average Price"
FROM ORDERS;

Output:

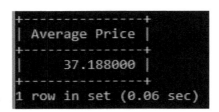

Practice Exercise 13-3

SELECT SUM(QUANTITY) AS "Total Quantity On Order"

FROM ORDERS

WHERE PRODUCTID = 101005;

Output:

```
+------------------------------+
| Total Quantity On Order      |
+------------------------------+
|                           61 |
+------------------------------+
1 row in set (0.04 sec)
```

Chapter 14: Implementing Database Integrity

Data integrity is one of the foremost concerns when using databases. You do not just set up a database to store data. You also want to ensure that the data are reliable, accurate, and consistent. Implementing and maintaining data integrity is necessary if you want your database to provide true and dependable information at all times.

Many scenarios could pose risks to data integrity. Here are some examples:

- A user may try to enter a response, which is not in the desired format. One example is entering a wrong format for a telephone number.
- A user may try to encode a date outside the specified range.
- An error or bug in a linked application tries to remove the wrong data.
- The network may go down while moving data from one database to another.
- The database administrator or developer mistakenly inserts the wrong data set of into a table.
- A developer accidentally enters test data into a running production system, which disrupts the operation.

- A user may try to delete a record, which is being used as a reference object in another table.
- A hacker manages to gain network access and removes the database and all stored data.
- A hacker successfully steals passwords from the database and modifies some information.
- A fire burns the network and database location.

Some threats can be handled inside the database by applying constraints. Some can be addressed by other database management features such as regular backing up of data and testing of backup files. Some will need non-database solutions such as maintaining an offsite backup location, implementing security policies, ensuring that the network is operating properly, and providing training to all users.

4 Types of Data Integrity

In the database world, data integrity is often categorized into the following types:

Row integrity

Referential integrity

Domain integrity

User-defined integrity

Row Integrity

Row integrity involves assigning a unique identifier for each row in a table. This identifier is used to tell each record and is usually called the table's Primary Key. A Primary Key may consist of one or more columns and may not be a NULL value.

Column integrity

Column Integrity specifies that all data to be stored in a column must follow the same definition and use the same format. Hence, all column values must have the same data type, default value, length, range, and other attributes.

If you try, for example, to enter a decimal value in a column specified as a VARCHAR type column, it will return an error. If you specify a column to be a VARCHAR column with maximum of 25 characters that cannot be NULL, you will run into errors if you enter values that are more than 25 characters or if you do not enter a value at all.

Referential Integrity

Referential integrity specifies that if a value is being used as a reference, it have to exist. This means that a record cannot be deleted or updated if it has been referenced by another process or value.

Referential integrity is defined during the database design phase. It is implemented by establishing relationships between tables. Once the referential relationship is created, the database engine will enforce the referential integrity rules and flag violations by returning errors.

User-defined integrity

User-defined Integrity rules are implemented in cases where the column integrity, referential integrity, and row integrity are insufficient to ensure the smooth operation of a database. Some businesses, for example, use complex applications that require more protection to ensure that data are stored securely, correctly, and consistently. They may be using applications that are based on biometrics data to avoid unauthorized intrusion on the database files.

Some users may use techniques like database triggers, functions, or stored procedures. Some uses external tools or non-SQL languages.

Applying Constraints

Constraints are the rules or restrictions that will be applied on a table or its columns. These rules are applied to ensure that only specific data types can be entered on a table. Using constraints, helps ensure the accuracy and reliability of data.

You can specify constraints on a table or column level. When constraints are specified on a column level, they are only applicable to a specific column. When they are defined on a table basis, they are implemented on the entire table.

SQL offers several types of constraints. Following are the most commonly used ones:

PRIMARY Key
FOREIGN Key

UNIQUE Key

DEFAULT Constraint

CHECK Constraint

INDEX

NOT NULL

PRIMARY Key

A Primary Key is a unique value, which identifies a row or record. A table can only have one primary key but it may consist of several fields. A column that had been identified specified, as the primary key cannot have NULL values. Generally, you would designate a primary at the time a table is created. It is also possible to specify a primary key later with the ALTER TABLE command.

Creating a Primary Key

This statement creates the SUPPLIER'S table and specifies the ID field as the primary key:

CREATE TABLE SUPPLIERS(

ID INT NOT NULL,

```
        FNAME VARCHAR(30) NOT NULL,
        LNAME VARCHART (25) NOT NULL,
        AGE INT NOT NULL,
        ADDRESS (VARCHAR(50),
        SALARY DECIMAL (12, 2),
        PRIMARY KEY (ID)
);
```

You may also specify a primary key constraint later using the ALTER TABLE statement. Here is the code for adding a primary constraint to the EMPLOYEES table:

```
ALTER TABLE SALES
ADD CONSTRAINTS PRIMARY (INVOICENO);
```

Deleting Primary Key Constraint

To remove the primary key constraint from a table, you will use the ALTER TABLE with the DROP statement.

For examples, to delete the Primary Key in the SALES table, you will use this statement:

```
ALTER TABLE SALES DROP PRIMARY KEY;
```

FOREIGN Key

A foreign key or referencing key constraint is used to associate a table with another table. It is commonly used when you are working on parent and child tables. In this type of table relationship, a key in the child table points to a primary key in the parent table.

A foreign key may consist of one or several columns containing values that match the primary key in another table. It is commonly used to ensure referential integrity within the database.

The following example shows the table structures for the PRODUCTS table and ORDERS table.

PRODUCTS Table

Field	Type	Null	Key
PRODUCTID	int(6)	NO	PRI
PRODNAME	varchar(30)	YES	
PRICE	dec...l(9...	YES	
INSTOCK	int(7)	...ES	
ONORDER	int(7)		

ORDERS Table

Field	Type	Null	Key
ORDERNO	int(8)	NO	PRI
ORDERDATE	date	YES	
PRODUCTID	int(6)	YES	
QUANTITY	int(6)	YES	
PRICE	decimal(9,2)	YES	

The PRODUCTS Table contains basic information about all products in the database. It uses the PRODUCTID as its primary key to provide unique identification for each product. The ORDERS table contains information about all orders issued to suppliers. It uses the column ORDERNO as its primary key.

Notice that the ORDERS table does not have a column for Product Name but it does have a column for PRODUCTID. The PRODUCTID is a common identifier for the PRODUCTS and ORDERS table. It will serve as a referencing key between the two tables. The PRODUCTID is the primary key in the PRODUCTS table and it is the FOREIGN key in the ORDERS table.

UNIQUE Key

A UNIQUE key constraint is used when you want to make sure that all column values are unique. The Unique key constraint prevents two or more rows from holding the same values in a column.

For example, you can apply this constraint if you do not want two or more products to have the same description in the PRODUCTS table:

```
CREATE TABLE PRODUCTS(
    PRODUCTID INT(6) NOT NULL,
    PRODNAME VARCHAR(30) NOT NULL UNIQUE,
    PRICE DECIMAL(9,2),
    INSTOCK(7),
    ONORDER(7),
    PRIMARY KEY(PRODUCTID),
    );
```

For existing tables, you can use the ALTER TABLE statement to add a UNIQUE key constraint.

For example, to add a UNIQUE key to the PRODUCTS table, you can use this statement:

```
ALTER TABLE PRODUCTS
    MODIFY PRODNAME VARCHAR(30) NOT NULL, UNIQUE;
```

If you want to apply the Unique constraint to more than one column at a time, you can use the ALTER TABLE with the ADD CONSTRAINT clause.

For example, to add the unique key on both Product Name and Price, you will use this statement:

```
ALTER TABLE PRODUCTS
    ADD CONSTRAINT myUniqueConstraint UNIQUE(PRODNAME, PRICE);
```

Removing a UNIQUE constraint

To remove the myUniqueConstraint above, you can use the ALTER TABLE with the DROP statement:

```
ALTER TABLE PRODUCTS
    DROP CONSTRAINT myUnique Constraint;
```

DEFAULT Constraint

The DEFAULT constraint is used to specify a default value when the users fails to enter a value for a column while adding data or performing an INSERT INTO operation.

For example, the following statement will create the EMPLOYEES table. Take note that the SALARY column is assigned a default value of 3000.00. This value will be applied if the user does not provide a value when adding new records.

```
CREATE TABLE EMPLOYEES(
    ID INT NOT NULL,
    FNAME VARCHAR(20) NOT NULL,
    LNAME VARCHAR(20) NOT NULL,
    ADDRESSS VARCHAR(50),
    CITY VARCHAR(25),
    STATE VARCHAR(25),
    SALARY DECIMAL(12,2) DEFAULT 3000.00,
    PRIMARY KEY(ID)
    );
```

You can also use the ALTER TABLE statement with the MODIFY clause to apply a DEFAULT constraint to an existing table.

Example:

```
ALTER TABLE EMPLOYEES
    MODIFY SALARY DECIMAL(12,2) DEFAULT 3000.00;
```

Removing a Default Constraint

To remove a DEFAULT constraint, you can use the ALTER TABLE statement with the DROP command.

Example:

```
ALTER TABLE EMPLOYEES
    DROP COLUMN SALARY DEFAULT;
```

CHECK Constraint

A CHECK constraint is used to ensure that all values placed in a column satisfy the given condition. Attempting to enter a data that violates the condition will result to the violation of the CHECK constraint. In turn, it will cause rejection of the data.

For example, the following statement will create the MEMBERS table.

```
CREATE TABLE MEMBERS
    ID INT(6) NOT NULL,
    FIRST_NAME(20) NOT NULL,
    LAST_NAME(20) NOT NULL,
    AGE INT(3) NOT NULL CHECK (AGE >= 18),
    GROUP VARCHAR(15),
    PRIMARY KEY(ID)
);
```

The above statement applies a CHECK constraint on the AGE column by specifying that the value should be equal to or more than 18.

You will use the ALTER TABLE statement with the MODIFY clause to add a CHECK constraint to a column of an existing table.

Example:

ALTER TABLE MEMBERS
    MODIFY AGE INT(3) NOT NULL CHECK(AGE>=18);

INDEX Constraint

The INDEX constraint is used to build and access information quickly from a database. You can create an index using one or more columns. Once the INDEX is created, a ROWID is assigned to each before a sort operation. Proper indexing enhances the performance of databases.

Syntax:

```
CREATE INDEX index_name
    ON table_name(column1, column2 column3...);
```

For instance, if you regularly search for a set of employees from a specific state, you may want to create an INDEX on the state column.

Here is the statement:

```
CREATE INDEX idx_state
    ON EMPLOYEES(STATE);
```

Removing the INDEX Constraint

To remove the INDEX Constraint, you can use the ALTER TABLE statement with the DROP command.

For example, to remove the idx_state INDEX constraint on the EMPLOYEES table, you will use this statement:

```
ALTER TABLE EMPLOYEES
DROP INDEX idx_state;
```

The NOT NULL Constraint

The "NULL" value refers to an undefined or unknown value. NULL values are not the same as zeroes, empty strings, blanks, or default values. It indicates the lack of value.

Columns take NULL value by default. This is called the nullability attribute. If you want to override the NULL default value, you will have to apply the NOT NULL constraint. This constraint prevents the database engine from taking NULL values. Using the NULL constraint prevents NULL values from populating your tables.

To illustrate, the following statement creates the STUDENTS table with seven columns:

```
CREATE TABLE STUDENTS
  ID INT(8) NOT NULL,
  FIRSTNAME VARCHAR (25) NOT NULL,
  LASTNAME VARCHAR(25) NOT NULL,
  YEAR_LEVEL VARCHAR(15) NOT NULL,
  ADDRESS VARCHAR(50),
  CITY VARCHAR(20),
  STATE VARCHAR(20),
  PRIMARY KEY(ID),
);
```

Notice that the NOT NULL constraint was applied on the ID, FIRSTNAME, LASTNAME, and YEAR_LEVEL columns. This means that these columns will not take NULL values.

Later on, you may decide to add a NOT NULL constrain on the STATE column. You can use the ALTER TABLE statement with the MODIFY command for that purpose.

```
ALTER TABLE STUDENTS
  MODIFY STATE VARCHAR(20) NOT NULL;
```

Summary

Data integrity refers to the reliability, accuracy, and consistency of database information. There are four main areas of data integrity: row integrity, referential integrity, domain integrity, and user-defined integrity. Constraints are the restrictions applied on a table to screen data entry and ensure that only the specified types are recorded. SQL supports several types of constraints such as PRIMARY key, FOREIGN key, UNIQUE key, DEFAULT constraint, INDEX, and NOT NULL constraints.

Chapter 15: Views

In the previous chapters, you have learned that tables are used to hold data. Views can be considered as virtual tables that do not contain data. Their content is defined though a query.

A view is created by an SQL statement that associates the name of a view and its content to an actual table. It can contain the entire rows of a table or some specified rows from tables. You can create one or multiple tables subject to the SQL query definition.

There are several advantages for using views. For one, views can serve as a form of security by limiting users' access to specific rows or columns. In addition, they can be used to return a selective number of data instead of detailed reports. Views are also useful for summarizing information from multiple tables. They help structure data naturally and intuitively.

Unlike a stored procedure, views do not use parameters to perform functions.
Views can be a simple view or complex view.

A simple view is one, which is generated from a single table, does not store groups of data, and has no functions.

A complex table is generated from a single or multiple tables, stores groups of data, and has functions.

Creating Views

You can create views from another view, multiple tables, or a single table using the CREATE VIEW statement.

A user must possess the proper system privilege to crate views.

Below is the basic syntax for creating a view:

```
CREATE VIEW view_name AS
SELECT column1, column2.....
FROM table_name
WHERE [condition];
```

You may also specify more than one table in the SELECT statement.

To see how the CREATE VIEW statement works, you will be using the EMPLOYEES table from the steelcompany with the following data:

EMP_NO	FNAME	LNAME	DEPARTMENT	SALARY
11	Janice	Winkle	Sales	5000.00
12	Alan	Mars	Sales	3000.00
13	Michelle	Pars	Finance	4000.00
14	Andrew	Winters	Finance	5000.00
15	Erma	Gherd	HR	5000.00
16	Julius	Hanes	Sales	2000.00
17	Arnold	Givens	HR	4000.00
18	Anthony	Wilson	Sales	3000.00
19	Megan	Jung	Finance	3000.00
20	Shane	Paulsen	Sales	3500.00

To create a view that will display the employee number, last name, and department from the EMPLOYEES table, you will use the following statement:

CREATE VIEW EMPLOYEES_VIEW AS
SELECT EMP_NO, FNAME, LNAME, DEPARTMENT
FROM EMPLOYEES;

At this point, you have created a virtual table named EMPLOYEES_VIEW. You can view its content by using the SELECT statement in the same that you would run a query on a normal table.

To view the EMPLOYEES_VIEW table, you can use this query statement:

SELECT * FROM EMPLOYEES_VIEW;

Output:

```
+----------+-----------+-----------+-------------+----------+
| EMP_NO   | FNAME     | LNAME     | DEPARTMENT  | SALARY   |
+----------+-----------+-----------+-------------+----------+
| 11       | Janice    | Winkle    | Sales       | 5000.00  |
| 12       | Alan      | Mars      | Sales       | 3000.00  |
| 13       | Michelle  | Pars      | Finance     | 4000.00  |
| 14       | Andrew    | Winters   | Finance     | 5000.00  |
| 15       | Erma      | Gherd     | HR          | 5000.00  |
| 16       | Julius    | Hanes     | Sales       | 2000.00  |
| 17       | Arnold    | Givens    | HR          | 4000.00  |
| 18       | Anthony   | Wilson    | Sales       | 3000.00  |
| 19       | Megan     | Jung      | Finance     | 3000.00  |
| 20       | Shane     | Paulsen   | Sales       | 3500.00  |
+----------+-----------+-----------+-------------+----------+
10 rows in set (0.02 sec)
```

The query on the EMPLOYEES_VIEW returned a table showing only the employee's number, last name, and department. The first name and salary columns from the original EMPLOYEES table were omitted from the view. This database feature is highly useful for protecting confidential information that should not be available to everyone.

Using the WITH CHECK OPTION

The WITH CHECK OPTION is an option or modifier in the CEATE VIEW statement. This option is used to ensure that INSERTs and UPDATE commands match the conditions specified in the CREATE VIEW specifications. The INSERT or UPDATE commands raise an error if the conditions are not met.

The following statement is an example of the CHECK OPTION:

```
CREATE VIEW EMPLOYEES_VIEW AS
SELECT EMP_ID, LNAME,
DEPARTMENT
FROM EMPLOYEES
WHERE LNAME IS NOT NULL
WITH CHECK OPTION;
```

In the above statement, the WITH CHECK OPTION is used to reject the insertion of any NULL values in the LNAME column of the VIEW.

Updating a View

The UPDATE operation in VIEW is similar to the UPDATE operation in tables. However, be aware that that updating a view will also update the data in the base table.

Syntax:

```
UPDATE view-name SET VALUE
WHERE condition;
```

The UPDATE VIEW operation is subject to some conditions. You should be aware of these restrictions if you want to avoid issues with data integrity and constraints violations.

Here are some of the rules you have to consider when performing an UPDATE VIEW operation:

The DISTINCT keyword should not be used in the SELECT clause.

The GROUP BY or HAVING modifiers may not be included in the query.

Set functions should not be included in the SELECT clause.

Summary functions should not be included in the SELECT clause.

An ORDER BY clause may not be included within the SELECT clause.

Set operators should not be used within the SELECT clause.

Subqueries are not allowed in the WHERE clause.

You can only specify one table in the FROM clause.

You may not update calculated columns.

The INSERT query will only work if all columns specified as NOT NULL in the source table are also part of the VIEW.

Make sure that the abovementioned conditions are satisfied before executing an update on a view.

To demonstrate the UPDATE operation, you will be using the EMPLOYEES_VIEW shown above with the following data:

```
+--------+----------+---------+------------+---------+
| EMP_NO | FNAME    | LNAME   | DEPARTMENT | SALARY  |
+--------+----------+---------+------------+---------+
| 11     | Janice   | Winkle  | Sales      | 5000.00 |
| 12     | Alan     | Mars    | Sales      | 3000.00 |
| 13     | Michelle | Pars    | Finance    | 4000.00 |
| 14     | Andrew   | Winters | Finance    | 5000.00 |
| 15     | Erma     | Gherd   | HR         | 5000.00 |
| 16     | Julius   | Hanes   | Sales      | 2000.00 |
| 17     | Arnold   | Givens  | HR         | 4000.00 |
| 18     | Anthony  | Wilson  | Sales      | 3000.00 |
| 19     | Megan    | Jung    | Finance    | 3000.00 |
| 20     | Shane    | Paulsen | Sales      | 3500.00 |
+--------+----------+---------+------------+---------+
10 rows in set (0.02 sec)
```

Assuming you want to update the DEPARTMENT for the employee with the surname Paulsen, the statement would be:

UPDATE EMPLOYEES_VIEW

SET DEPARTMENT = 'Finance'

WHERE LNAME = 'Paulsen';

To view the updated EMPLOYEES_VIEW TABLE:

SELECT * FROM EMPLOYEES_VIEW;

Output:

```
+---------+----------+---------+------------+
| EMP_NO  | FNAME    | LNAME   | DEPARTMENT |
+---------+----------+---------+------------+
| 11      | Janice   | Winkle  | Sales      |
| 12      | Alan     | Mars    | Sales      |
| 13      | Michelle | Pars    | Finance    |
| 14      | Andrew   | Winters | Finance    |
| 15      | Erma     | Gherd   | HR         |
| 16      | Julius   | Hanes   | Sales      |
| 17      | Arnold   | Givens  | HR         |
| 18      | Anthony  | Wilson  | Sales      |
| 19      | Megan    | Jung    | Finance    |
| 20      | Shane    | Paulsen | Finance    |
+---------+----------+---------+------------+
10 rows in set (0.00 sec)
```

Take note that the EMPLOYEES_VIEW was updated and the UPDATE operation changed Paulsen's department from 'Sales' to 'Finance'.

We can check the base table to see the impact of the UPDATE command you have just executed:

SELECT * FROM EMPLOYEES;

Output:

```
+---------+----------+----------+------------+----------+
| EMP_NO  | FNAME    | LNAME    | DEPARTMENT | SALARY   |
+---------+----------+----------+------------+----------+
| 11      | Janice   | Winkle   | Sales      | 5000.00  |
| 12      | Alan     | Mars     | Sales      | 3000.00  |
| 13      | Michelle | Pars     | Finance    | 4000.00  |
| 14      | Andrew   | Winters  | Finance    | 5000.00  |
| 15      | Erma     | Gherd    | HR         | 5000.00  |
| 16      | Julius   | Hanes    | Sales      | 2000.00  |
| 17      | Arnold   | Givens   | HR         | 4000.00  |
| 18      | Anthony  | Wilson   | Sales      | 3000.00  |
| 19      | Megan    | Jung     | Finance    | 3000.00  |
| 20      | Shane    | Paulsen  | Finance    | 3500.00  |
+---------+----------+----------+------------+----------+
10 rows in set (0.03 sec)
```

The result shows that the UPDATE operation on the VIEW table also changed the data in the source table.

Inserting Rows into a View

Like the UPDATE command, the INSERT command may also be used in a VIEW. You can insert rows into a view using the same rules and conditions you have learned earlier for the UPDATE command.

To see how the INSERT INTO works, you can try inserting the following data to the EMPLOYEES_VIEW:

EMP_NO   21
FNAME   Philip
LNAME   Martin
DEPARTMENT   Sales

You can use this statement:

INSERT INTO EMPLOYEES_VIEW (EMP_NO, FNAME, LNAME, DEPARTMENT)
VALUES(21, 'Philip, 'Martin', 'Sales');

The INSERT INTO statement will work in the EMPLOYEES_VIEW because all columns with NOT NULL definitions were included in the view.

To view the updated EMPLOYEES_VIEW table:

SELECT * FROM EMPLOYEES_VIEW;

Output:

```
+--------+----------+---------+------------+
| EMP_NO | FNAME    | LNAME   | DEPARTMENT |
+--------+----------+---------+------------+
| 11     | Janice   | Winkle  | Sales      |
| 12     | Alan     | Mars    | Sales      |
| 13     | Michelle | Pars    | Finance    |
| 14     | Andrew   | Winters | Finance    |
| 15     | Erma     | Gherd   | HR         |
| 16     | Julius   | Hanes   | Sales      |
| 17     | Arnold   | Givens  | HR         |
| 18     | Anthony  | Wilson  | Sales      |
| 19     | Megan    | Jung    | Finance    |
| 20     | Shane    | Paulsen | Finance    |
| 21     | Philip   | Martin  | Sales      |
+--------+----------+---------+------------+
11 rows in set (0.00 sec)
```

The EMPLOYEES_VIEW now has 11 rows of data.

To check the effect of the INSERT INTO statement on the EMPLOYEES_VIEW to its source table, the EMPLOYEES table, you can run this query:

SELECT * FROM EMPLOYEES;

Output:

```
+--------+----------+---------+------------+----------+
| EMP_NO | FNAME    | LNAME   | DEPARTMENT | SALARY   |
+--------+----------+---------+------------+----------+
| 11     | Janice   | Winkle  | Sales      | 5000.00  |
| 12     | Alan     | Mars    | Sales      | 3000.00  |
| 13     | Michelle | Pars    | Finance    | 4000.00  |
| 14     | Andrew   | Winters | Finance    | 5000.00  |
| 15     | Erma     | Gherd   | HR         | 5000.00  |
| 16     | Julius   | Hanes   | Sales      | 2000.00  |
| 17     | Arnold   | Givens  | HR         | 4000.00  |
| 18     | Anthony  | Wilson  | Sales      | 3000.00  |
| 19     | Megan    | Jung    | Finance    | 3000.00  |
| 20     | Shane    | Paulsen | Finance    | 3500.00  |
| 21     | Philip   | Martin  | Sales      | NULL     |
+--------+----------+---------+------------+----------+
11 rows in set (0.02 sec)
```

The INSERT INTO operation on the EMPLOYEES_VIEW also updated the EMPLOYEES table. Notice that SALARY, the only hidden column, shows a NULL value for the new row of data. In the real world, another employee could be handling the function of encoding or updating confidential information like the employees' salary.

Deleting Rows From a View

It is also possible to delete rows from a VIEW. The rules and conditions for the UPDATE and INSERT commands for a view apply to the DELETE command.

For example, to delete the record for employee number 20, you can write this statement:

DELETE FROM EMPLOYEES_VIEW
WHERE EMP_NO = 20;

Here is the updated EMPLOYEES_VIEW:

```
+----------+----------+----------+------------+----------+
| EMP_NO   | FNAME    | LNAME    | DEPARTMENT | SALARY   |
+----------+----------+----------+------------+----------+
| 11       | Janice   | Winkle   | Sales      | 5000.00  |
| 12       | Alan     | Mars     | Sales      | 3000.00  |
| 13       | Michelle | Pars     | Finance    | 4000.00  |
| 14       | Andrew   | Winters  | Finance    | 5000.00  |
| 15       | Erma     | Gherd    | HR         | 5000.00  |
| 16       | Julius   | Hanes    | Sales      | 2000.00  |
| 17       | Arnold   | Givens   | HR         | 4000.00  |
| 18       | Anthony  | Wilson   | Sales      | 3000.00  |
| 19       | Megan    | Jung     | Finance    | 3000.00  |
| 21       | Philip   | Martin   | Sales      |     NULL |
+----------+----------+----------+------------+----------+
10 rows in set (0.05 sec)
```

The updated EMPLOYEES_VIEW shows that the data for employee number 20 has been deleted.

Let us see how this affects the EMPLOYEES table:

SELECT * FROM EMPLOYEES;

Output:

```
+---------+-----------+----------+------------+----------+
| EMP_NO  | FNAME     | LNAME    | DEPARTMENT | SALARY   |
+---------+-----------+----------+------------+----------+
| 11      | Janice    | Winkle   | Sales      | 5000.00  |
| 12      | Alan      | Mars     | Sales      | 3000.00  |
| 13      | Michelle  | Pars     | Finance    | 4000.00  |
| 14      | Andrew    | Winters  | Finance    | 5000.00  |
| 15      | Erma      | Gherd    | HR         | 5000.00  |
| 16      | Julius    | Hanes    | Sales      | 2000.00  |
| 17      | Arnold    | Givens   | HR         | 4000.00  |
| 18      | Anthony   | Wilson   | Sales      | 3000.00  |
| 19      | Megan     | Jung     | Finance    | 3000.00  |
| 21      | Philip    | Martin   | Sales      |    NULL  |
+---------+-----------+----------+------------+----------+
10 rows in set (0.06 sec)
```

The DELETE command on the EMPLOYEES_VIEW also caused the removal of a row of data from the EMPLOYEES table, its source table.

Dropping Views

When a view has outlived its usefulness, you may decide to remove it from your database. You can easily do so with a simple DROP statement:

DROP VIEW view_name;

For example, if you want to remove the EMPLOYEES_VIEW, you will use this statement:

DROP VIEW EMPLOYEES_VIEW;

The database will return an error if you try to access the EMPLOYEES_VIEW at this point.

Unlike the UPDATE, INSERT, and DELETE statements, a DROP VIEW operation has no impact on the source table.

Read-Only VIEW

The Read-Only option is used to limit access to a VIEW.

Syntax:

CREATE or REPLACE FORCE VIEW view_name AS

```
SELECT column_name(s)
FROM table_name
WHERE condition WITH read-only;
```

Summary

Views are virtual tables, which are defined through a query. Views do not contain data. Using views offer many advantages such as providing a form of security by limiting the users' access to certain data. They can help make data retrieval more efficient by limiting the display to a range of data or columns. They provide a simple and natural way of structuring data and are useful for summarizing data from several tables.

Practice Exercises

Practice Exercise 15-1

This exercise will use the following EMPLOYEES_RECORD table:

```
+--------+--------------------+---------+----------------+
| ID     | AGENT              | SALARY  | BRANCH         |
+--------+--------------------+---------+----------------+
| 16015  | Patricia McMilian  | 9500.00 | Arizona        |
| 17021  | Lola Bowker        | 9500.00 | Utah           |
| 17024  | Robert Hamson      | 9500.00 | Michigan       |
| 17050  | Brent Ringer       | 9500.00 | Illinois       |
| 17088  | Judy Wilson        | 9500.00 | Arizona        |
| 18017  | Daryl Philips      | 9500.00 | Utah           |
| 18024  | Kathleen Rivers    | 9500.00 | Ohio           |
| 18058  | John Harrison      | 9500.00 | Georgia        |
| 18064  | Alex Mosley        | 9500.00 | Illinois       |
| 18075  | Greg Kendall       | 9500.00 | Washington     |
| 18094  | Brian Martin       | 9500.00 | Colorado       |
| 19015  | Russel Harris      | 9500.00 | Maryland       |
| 19023  | Richard Foulks     | 9500.00 | Washington     |
| 19025  | Susan Taylor       | 9500.00 | Florida        |
| 19033  | James Roberson     | 6500.00 | South Carolina |
| 19048  | Alice Perkins      | 5000.00 | Michigan       |
| 19065  | Michael Bourne     | 6000.00 | Ohio           |
+--------+--------------------+---------+----------------+
17 rows in set (0.39 sec)
```

Write a statement to create a view that will display the ID, AGENT, and BRANCH from the EMPLOYEES_RECORD table. You will name the view as EMPLOYEES_RECORD_VIEW.

Display the VIEW you have created.

Practice Exercise 15-2

Add the following data to the EMPLOYEES_RECORD_VIEW:

ID	AGENT	BRANCH
19070	Jimmy Hearns	Washington
19071	Scott Vioz	Georgia
19072	Gem Shand	Utah

Show the updated EMPLOYEES_RECORD_VIEW.

Solution

Practice Exercise 15-1

CREATE VIEW EMPLOYEES_RECORD_VIEW AS
SELECT ID, AGENT, BRANCH
FROM EMPLOYEES_RECORD;

SELECT * FROM EMPLOYEES_RECORD_VIEW;

Output:

```
+--------+-------------------+-----------------+
| ID     | AGENT             | BRANCH          |
+--------+-------------------+-----------------+
| 16015  | Patricia McMilian | Arizona         |
| 17021  | Lola Bowker       | Utah            |
| 17024  | Robert Hamson     | Michigan        |
| 17050  | Brent Ringer      | Illinois        |
| 17088  | Judy Wilson       | Arizona         |
| 18017  | Daryl Philips     | Utah            |
| 18024  | Kathleen Rivers   | Ohio            |
| 18058  | John Harrison     | Georgia         |
| 18064  | Alex Mosley       | Illinois        |
| 18075  | Greg Kendall      | Washington      |
| 18094  | Brian Martin      | Colorado        |
| 19015  | Russel Harris     | Maryland        |
| 19023  | Richard Foulks    | Washington      |
| 19025  | Susan Taylor      | Florida         |
| 19033  | James Roberson    | South Carolina  |
| 19048  | Alice Perkins     | Michigan        |
| 19065  | Michael Bourne    | Ohio            |
+--------+-------------------+-----------------+
17 rows in set (0.05 sec)
```

Practice Exercise 15-2

INSERT INTO EMPLOYEES_RECORD_VIEW

VALUES(19070, 'Jimmy Hearns', 'Washington);

INSERT INTO EMPLOYEES_RECORD_VIEW

VALUES(19071, 'Scott Vioz', 'Georgia');

INSERT INTO EMPLOYEES_RECORD_VIEW
VALUES(19072, 'Gem Shand', 'Utah');

SELECT * FROM EMPLOYEES_RECORD_VIEW;

Output:

```
+--------+------------------+-----------------+
| ID     | AGENT            | BRANCH          |
+--------+------------------+-----------------+
| 16015  | Patricia McMilian | Arizona        |
| 17021  | Lola Bowker      | Utah            |
| 17024  | Robert Hamson    | Michigan        |
| 17050  | Brent Ringer     | Illinois        |
| 17088  | Judy Wilson      | Arizona         |
| 18017  | Daryl Philips    | Utah            |
| 18024  | Kathleen Rivers  | Ohio            |
| 18058  | John Harrison    | Georgia         |
| 18064  | Alex Mosley      | Illinois        |
| 18075  | Greg Kendall     | Washington      |
| 18094  | Brian Martin     | Colorado        |
| 19015  | Russel Harris    | Maryland        |
| 19023  | Richard Foulks   | Washington      |
| 19025  | Susan Taylor     | Florida         |
| 19033  | James Roberson   | South Carolina  |
| 19048  | Alice Perkins    | Michigan        |
| 19065  | Michael Bourne   | Ohio            |
| 19070  | Jimmy Hearns     | Washington      |
| 19071  | Scott Vioz       | Georgia         |
| 19072  | Gem Shand        | Utah            |
+--------+------------------+-----------------+
20 rows in set (0.00 sec)
```

Chapter 16: Transactions

Transactions are sequences of tasks which are performed in a logical order against a database. A transaction is any action that creates changes to the database. It includes actions such as updating, deleting and adding a record to a database. Controlling transactions is essential if we want to manage database errors and maintain data integrity.

SQL transactions possess four attributes, which are denoted by the acronym ACID:

Atomicity   This property applies an "all" or "nothing" approach to work units. It requires the full completion of a work unit. If one or more operations fail to complete successfully, the transaction is terminated and all transactions are returned to their old state as if nothing happened.

Consistency   This property ensures that changes will occur in the database after every completed transaction.

Isolation   This property allows transactions to be performed independently of each other.

Durability   This property ensures that the effects of completed transactions will be preserved. This means that there will be no loss of data in the event of errors in the application or hardware.

Transaction Control Commands

The commands COMMIT, ROLLBACK, SAVEPOINT, and SET TRANSACTIONS are the commands used to manage SQL transactions.

Transactional control commands are used with the Data Manipulating Language such as UPDATE, INSERT, and DELETE. You cannot use these commands when constructing or dropping a table.

COMMIT

The COMMIT statement is used to save changes arising from the completion of a transaction. Its staring point is the last ROLLBACK or COMMIT

Syntax:

COMMIT;

ROLLBACK Command

This command is used to reverse unsaved transactions. You can only use it to reverse transactions that have not been committed or saved to a database. It can be used to reverse transactions from the last ROLLBACK or COMMIT point.

Syntax: ROLLBACK;

SAVEPOINT

This command is used to establish markers that can be used to perform Rollbacks. It's that part of the transaction that you can go back to without rolling back everything.

Syntax:

SAVEPOINT SAVEPOINT_NAME;

Following is the syntax for going back to the SAVEPOINT:

Syntax:

ROLLBACK TO SAVEPOINT_NAME;

Releasing Savepoint

The RELEASE SAVEPOINT command removes a SAVEPOINT.

Syntax:

RELEASE SAVEPOINT SAVEPOINT_NAME;

SET TRANSACTION

The SET TRANSACTION command is used to declare the attributes of a transaction. You can use this to initialize a database transaction. For example, this syntax declares the transaction that follows as either Read Write or Read Only:

SET TRANSACTION [READ WRITE | READ ONLY];

Chapter 17: Triggers

A trigger is a special stored procedure which is run automatically in response to a specific event such as delete, update, or insert. Database triggers are used to protect data integrity. They can be used to verify the content and changes in a table.

A trigger is formed by a set of SQL statements which are stored in the database catalog. It is executed each time a table-related event such as delete, update, or insert occurs.

In this chapter, you will learn about triggers and their implementation and limitations.

Creating Triggers

The CREATE TRIGGER statement is used to create a trigger.

Syntax:

```
CREATE TRIGGER trigger_name trigger_time trigger_event
ON table_name
FOR EACH ROW
BEGIN
...
END;
```

A trigger can only be invoked by a single event. The event can be a DELETE, UPDATE, or INSERT action. If you want to set up more than one event for a trigger, you will have to define several triggers to be assigned to each event.

You can specify the trigger activation time before or after. The activation time must be set whenever a trigger is defined. The BEFORE keyword is used if you want to set up a trigger that will execute actions prior to a change. The AFTER keyword is used if you have to execute actions after the changes have been executed.

Since the syntax requires a table name after the ON keyword, you will have to specify the table which will be linked to that trigger.

SQL statements are written between the BEGIN and END blocks.

A trigger name is specified right after the CREATE TRIGGER statement. Bear in mind that the name should comply with the naming convention.

Conclusion

I'd like to thank you and congratulate you for transiting my lines from start to finish.

I hope this book was able to help you to learn the fundamentals of SQL programming.

The next step is to take advance courses in SQL programming as well as database design and administration.

I wish you the best of luck!

By: Richard Numpy